THE CHIHUAHUA

Tammy Gagne

INTERPET
PUBLISHING

The Chihuahua

Project Team
Editor: Heather Russell-Revesz
Copy Editor: Carl Schutt
Indexer: Ann W. Truesdale
Design: Mary Ann Kahn
Series Design: Mada Design
Series Originator: Dominique De Vito

United Kingdom Editorial Team
Hannah Turner
Nicola Parker
Claire Cullinan

First published in the United Kingdom in 2008 by
Interpet Publishing
Vincent Lane
Dorking
Surrey
RH4 3YX

ISBN 978 1 84286 194 3

Printed and bound in Indonesia

This book has been published with the intent to provide accurate and authoritative information in regard to the subject matter within. While every reasonable precaution has been taken in preparation of this book, the author and publisher expressly disclaim responsibility for any errors, omissions, or adverse effects arising from the use or application of the information contained herein. The techniques and suggestions are used at the reader's discretion and are not to be considered a substitute for veterinary care. If you suspect a medical problem consult your veterinarian.

INTERPET
PUBLISHING

www.interpet.co.uk

TABLE OF CONTENTS

HISTORY
of the Chihuahua

The history of all dogs may be traced to one common ancestor—the wolf. Even the smallest breeds are directly linked to these larger canines. Although no true wolves inhabit South America, a small, dark subspecies called the Mexican grey wolf (*Canis lupus baileyi*) still exists in Mexico today. Sometimes referred to as *el lobo*, this is the animal from which many experts believe Chihuahuas descend.

For some reason—probably his diminutive size—the Chihuahua (pronounced Chih-WAH-waah) is often considered by the uninitiated to be somewhat less of a "real" dog than other canines. This is ironic, for when proper research is done, what is learned is that the Chihuahua is the oldest dog breed on the American continent, and in this sense, one of the most authentic of all dogs. Those who know the Chihuahua best, though, hardly need to be convinced of the breed's indisputable right to his place among the most remarkable of all canines, past and present.

EARLY DEVELOPMENT: A HISTORY RICH IN FOLKLORE

Although the Chihuahua will always be regarded as a bona fide Mexican, an assortment of contradicting theories suggest that the dog's origins might actually lie much farther away than in Mexico. Much is based on speculation, but the stories are undeniably compelling and have yet to be conclusively proven as either fact or fiction. It is unlikely we will ever know for sure which, if any, are true.

One intriguing theory is that the Chihuahua actually evolved from an animal that is native to Northern Africa called a fennec fox (*Fennecus zerda*). A member of the *Canidae* family, this obscure desert creature has huge ears and large, round eyes—closely resembling those of the Chihuahua. Weighing between only 3 and 3 1/2 pounds (1.4 and 1.6 kg), the fennec fox is often called the world's smallest canine. Like the Chihuahua, and unlike other foxes, fennecs are known to prefer the company of their own kind. They are one of the few fox species to live in groups.

Others insist that the Chihuahua is actually of European descent, more precisely from

Mexico is most likely the Chihuahua's country of origin.

International Image

The Chihuahua's image has graced the stamps of many nations throughout the world, including Antigua, Bulgaria, Cuba, Guyana, Nicaragua, Paraguay, Russia, Tanzania, and of course, Mexico.

Malta. A small breed of dog once existed on this island country, and like the Chihuahua this breed possessed a very unusual natural feature called a molera. This soft spot on the top of the skull is extremely rare in all other dog breeds. A related story tells how the mummified remains of a small dog bearing a molera was unearthed in an Egyptian tomb dating back approximately 3,000 years.

A very tangible piece of history that supports the European descent theory is a painting created in 1482 by the renowned artist named Alessandro Botticelli. This exquisite piece of art entitled "Scenes from the Life of Moses" graces the walls of the Sistine Chapel and depicts a dog remarkably similar to the Chihuahua—indicating that the breed may have existed in Europe long before Christopher Columbus first sailed to America a full decade later. If this theory is correct, the Spanish conquistadors were the ones to bring this unique dog with them to the New World.

Another common premise is that the Chihuahua originated in China. Known for successfully developing miniature dogs of various breeds, the Chinese could possibly have introduced the

Spaniards to the Chihuahua by way of trade. In this scenario the Spanish then brought the dogs with them to Mexico. After the Spanish destroyed the Aztec civilisation, the dogs would have been abandoned, left to the care of the natives who endured.

BREED HISTORY IN MEXICO

The most common and best-substantiated theory is that the Chihuahua's roots indeed lie in old Mexico. Archaeological evidence supports a history of the breed dating as far back as the fifth century C.E.—and suggests that the dog was not only present in central and southern regions of Mexico, but in South America, as well.

Members of the Toltec tribe, a culture that originated in northern Mexico and expanded throughout central and southern regions around 950 C.E., were known to have kept small dogs that were greatly revered. The breed was known as the Techichi. The Techichi had long hair and was a bit larger than the modern day Chihuahua. It is also rumoured to have been mute. Images of these

A Dog by Any Other Name

In Mexico the Chihuahua is known as el Chihuaheuno.

Chihuahuas were referred to as "Texas dogs" when they first came to the US in the late 19th century.

Columbus and the Chihuahua

Christopher Columbus may have encountered the Techichi, a probable ancestor of the Chihuahua, in the late 15th century on what is now the island of Cuba. In an historic letter to the king of Spain, Columbus wrote about having seen small dogs "which were mute and did not bark, as usual, but were domesticated."

dogs that greatly resemble the Chihuahua have been found in carvings from this period, including stones from the Pyramids of Cholula, predating 1530. When the Aztecs conquered the Toltecs, the Techichi continued their role as a symbol of wealth. Some families owned literally hundreds of these animals that were cared for and pampered by the families' slaves.

Archaeologists have found the Techichi alongside human remains in gravesites all over Mexico. When death was imminent, many individuals would request to be buried with their dogs. Although this may sound like a loving final gesture, it was actually a bit more self-serving in nature. A dog would be sacrificed upon his owner's death as part of a ritual to transfer the owner's sins to the dog, freeing the master's soul from responsibility of his previous actions and ensuring him a peaceful resting place. In some cases sculptures were used in place of an actual dog.

Sacrifices were a common practice of this time, and although it is difficult for our culture to understand, the Aztecs didn't consider their actions malevolent; on the contrary, they viewed the role of a sacrifice to be a great honour. Red-coloured dogs were usually used for this purpose. The extremely rare blue varieties, however, were regarded as sacred. To this day a blue Chihuahua is considered an exceptional treasure.

Yet another theory suggests that the Chihuahua we know today is a result of crossing the Techichi with Asiatic hairless dogs that lived on Spanish ships, who were kept as ratters at the time of the Spanish Conquest. Many breeders discard this assertion, however, due to the numerous differences in conformation between hairless breeds and the Chihuahua. Ultimately this, like all the other legends surrounding the Chihuahua, cannot be proven true or false.

BREED HISTORY IN THE UK

In the late 19th century representatives of the breed moved into Britain from the United States and directly from Mexico. In 1897, a Chihuahua was exhibited at the Ladies Kennel Club Show.

EARLY RECOGNITION

Technically the first Chihuahua to be recognised by the Kennel Club (KC) was registered in 1907, but another did not come along until 1924.

By the beginning of World War II, fewer than 100 dogs had been registered. The bombing and devastation that accompanied the war dramatically lessened these already conservative numbers, and by 1949 only eight registered dogs remained.

Fortunately, once homes were re-established, many sought the company of animals at the end of this dreadful period. With their compact size, tiny appetites, and charming personalities, Chihuahuas became a popular choice of canine companions. The breed's numbers began to rise again, with 111 Chihuahuas registered by 1953.

Due to a strike by electricians, the 1954 Crufts Dog Show was cancelled. As a result the first CCs were actually awarded by the Scottish Kennel Club at the Glasgow Show.

The breed was split into Longcoat and Smoothcoat by 1965 and 159 Smoothcoats and 87 Longcoats entered Crufts that year. Total numbers recorded at that time had reached over 3,000.

The first Chihuahua was registered with the American Kennel Club (AKC) in 1904. The dog was a stud fittingly named Midget. That same year four other Chihuahuas were also registered, and by 1915 a total of 30 Chihuahuas had bedcome official. Presently more than 40,000 Chihuahuas are registered each year with the AKC.

Long and short coat Chihuahuas were originally shown together–until the AKC divided them into two separate

The Establishment of Kennel Clubs

When dogfighting was outlawed in the 1830s and '40s, dog shows developed as a way for owners to display their dogs in a more positive way. The first organised event of this kind occurred in England in 1859; the first North American show was held in Quebec in 1867. With no breed standards as guidelines, however, judging was problematic. The rules seemed to be different at each show. There were also no standards for obedience within the ring, so mayhem frequently ensued.

The Kennel Club (KC) of Great Britain was established in 1873 as a means of registering official standards for each breed. The American Kennel Club (AKC) was founded in 1884, creating basic rules for the show ring.

Today kennel clubs are nonprofit making organisations whose members work together to create and uphold standards for all dog-related issues, including the registry and showing of purebred dogs. There are many such clubs in countries throuhout the world, but the KC and the AKC remain two of the most prominet and influential.

Awareness of the Chihuahua has increased this breed's popularity immensely over the years.

varieties in 1952. While still shown separately, today the two varieties are interbred, often producing a mixture of pups within a single litter. Whether short or long coat the conformation and character of the Chihuahua remains the same.

MODERN DAY CHIHUAHUA

Today we have a Toy dog that is a wonderful companion, and is small enough to accompany us almost everywhere. He is exceptionally loyal to his owners, and despite his size, he makes a great guard dog, as he will be quick to bark if strangers approach. He is often described as having terrier-like qualities, and this is often evident in his fearless, outgoing nature.

From Obscurity to Champions

1850: First Chihuahuas discovered by American archaeologists in the Mexican state of Chihuahua

1884: American tourists begin buying Chihuahuas in border markets of Mexico

1904: First Chihuahua registered by the AKC

1907: First Chihuahua registered by the KC

1928: First Chihuahua registered by the CKC

1949: The British Chihuahua Club formed

1951: First Chihuahua awarded Best in Show by AKC (Ch. Attas' Gretchen)

1975: First Long-coat Chihuahua awarded Best in Show by AKC (Ch. Snow Bunny d'Casa de Cris)

STILL MAKING HISTORY

In recent years the Chihuahua has become tremendously popular. But not everyone involved with the breed sees this sharp rise in demand as a good thing. Use of the Chihuahua's image in advertising for fast food and designer clothing, as well as the dog's presence alongside an increasing number of celebrities both on and off screen, have catapulted this tiny canine to star status. Whenever pop culture attaches itself to an animal, that animal then becomes a hot commodity, but this can often lead to thousands of unwanted animals left in re-homing centres when the "trend" is over.

Chihuahuas, although unquestionably cute and compact, are indeed real dogs with the same needs as any other canine pet. A dog should never be purchased as a mere accessory or because so-and-so has one. Buy a Chihuahua because you want a dog to love and care for, and you will have a very dear friend for many years.

Yo Quiero Taco Bell!

The most famous Chihuahua of the new millennium in the US is Gidget, the dog featured in the mammoth ad campaign of the popular fast food chain in the US, Taco Bell. While few can deny the charisma of the company's voiced-over Mexican mascot, Gidget is not your typical Chihuahua. With wider-set eyes, a longer snout, and abnormally long ears (commonly referred to as a deer type Chihuahua), the Taco Bell dog does not conform to the official standard for the breed.

2

CHARACTERISTICS
of the Chihuahua

C hihuahua owners love their dogs for many reasons—including, of course, their darling appearance. With their generously proportioned ears and animated expressions, Chihuahuas immediately capture the attention of all around them. Available in either a smooth or long coat variety, this compact dog has an expansive appeal.

SIZE AND GAIT

Chihuahuas move with a gracefulness unique to their breed. At first glance you might attribute this fluidity to the dog's size, but you soon discover that it has much more to do with charisma than stature. His gait is confident and strong, with his front and back legs in a driven synchronicity. Chihuahuas are both literally and figuratively light on their feet.

The Chihuahua is a well-balanced dog that, like many other breeds, is slightly longer than he is tall. Males are preferred to be slightly shorter than females, since it is important for females to have additional room for carrying puppies. There is actually no official scale issued by the KC for height, but an adult dog should weigh no more than 6 pounds (2.7 kg).

HEAD

Just as distinctive as the breed's size is his round, apple-domed head. Though not present in all dogs, many Chihuahuas have a soft spot on the top centre of their heads, similar to a human baby's fontanel. Called the molera, this small area that varies in both size and shape has an approximately 50 percent chance of closing completely by the time the dog is three years old. Very few moleras that do not close are large, but extra care should be given to protect the head when the bones have not completely fused.

At one time moleras were so prevalent that Chihuahuas without this feature were often considered suspect. More recently a link between the presence of a molera and a serious affliction called hydrocephalus (fluid on the brain) has been suggested. While dogs suffering from hydrocephalus commonly have large or open moleras, advanced research has revealed that a dog bearing a molera is not predisposed to this condition.

Chihuahuas come in both short- and long-coated varieties.

EYES

Pert and discerning, the Chihuahua's eyes complete the dog's saucy expression. Although white or blonde dogs may have lighter eyes, all other Chihuahuas' eyes should be dark or ruby coloured. Set wide apart, they should be round and full, but not protruding.

EARS

The Chihuahua would somehow be less Chihuahua without his large pointed ears that stand erect when alert and flare to the sides at 45 degree angles when the dog is relaxed.

Chihuahuas are born with delightfully floppy ears that begin to stand gradually over the dog's first few months of life. The actual age the ears will stand fully varies from pup to pup. It may be as early as eight weeks or as late as four months. It is not at all uncommon for either one or both ears to reach standing and then lower once again during teething. Ears that flop for this reason will resume an erect position when teething concludes, but ears that have never stood upright by the age of six months will likely never stand. Flopping ears will not cause your Chihuahua any discomfort, although they will prevent your dog from being shown.

MUZZLE

The muzzle is moderately short and somewhat pointed, and the nose may be one of several different colours, depending on the colouring of the individual dog. Blonde Chihuahuas most often have either self-coloured or black noses, but pink is also deemed acceptable for showing. The nose is self-coloured in moles, blues, and chocolates. Teeth should be arranged in a level or scissors bite.

BODY

A Chihuahua's elegant neck slopes smoothly into lean shoulders that slope further into a level back. The ribs are rounded, but shouldn't appear barrel shaped. Legs are straight under a strong chest. A Chihuahua has a sickle tail, which means it is carried up and out in a semicircle. The tip may or may not lightly brush the dog's back. This is a fine-boned yet muscular dog. The overall appearance should project subtle strength. Feet are small and dainty. The toes are well split up, but not spread. The pads are cushioned.

COAT

Short coats should lie close to the body, be soft to the touch, and appear glossy. A ruff on the neck is preferred, but it should be less abundant on the head and ears. The hair on a smooth coat's tail, however, is preferred furry.

Long coats should also be soft and for this variety, either flat or slightly curly. An undercoat is preferred. The dog's ears should be

Fédération Cynologique Internationale

While many people have only heard of the American Kennel Club, Kennel Club, and perhaps some other national kennel clubs, an international organisation actually exists. The Fédération Cynologique Internationale is the World Canine Organisation, which includes 80 members and contract partners (one member per country), each of which issues its own pedigrees and trains its own judges. The founding nations were Germany, Austria, Belgium, France, and the Netherlands. It was first formed in 1911 but later disappeared during World War I. The organisation was reconstituted in 1921. Currently, neither the United States nor Canada is a member.

The FCI ensures that its pedigrees and judges are organised by all FCI members. Every member country conducts international shows as well as working trials; results are sent to the FCI office, where they are input into computers. When a dog has been awarded a certain number of awards, he can receive the title of International Beauty or Working Champion. These titles are confirmed by the FCI.

The FCI organises 331 dog breeds, and each of them is the "property" of a specific country, ideally the one in which the breed developed. The owner countries of the breeds write the standard of these breeds in cooperation with the Standards and Scientific Commissions of the FCI, and the translation and updating are carried out by the FCI. In addition, via the national canine organisation and the FCI, every breeder can ask for international protection of his or her kennel name.

Obtaining a show-quality Chihuahua often requires a longer wait than for a pet-quality dog.

fringed. If heavier fringe is the sole reason for an ear's slight tipping, it will be excused in the ring, but weak ear leather will not. A show dog's ears should never be down. The tail should be plumed, both full and long. A bobtail will render a dog disqualified. Feathering is also preferred, along with a large ruff on the neck. Long coats are faulted for thin coats that resemble bareness.

Chihuahuas of both varieties of coats are often littermates. All pups are born with smooth coats, but they may be differentiated as early as three to four weeks of age. Around this time a very faint ridge appears down the back of a long coat. The coat will not fully develop for at least another year, though.

COLOUR

Available in a wide array of colours, markings, and splashes (all of which are considered acceptable by the KC), Chihuahuas can be found in white, black, and nearly everything in between. No one colour or set of markings should be judged as any better than another, but preferences outside the ring often exist.

WEIGHT

Weighing roughly the same amount as a bag of sugar, this breed often captivates fanciers with his tiny size. Unfortunately, there is no official minimum weight standard for this breed, and the cute factor has inspired some to breed Chihuahuas that sometimes fall within a dangerously low weight range—less than 2 pounds (.9 kg) in some instances. Certainly, all breeds may be born in a range of sizes. A smaller Chihuahua may be part of any litter belonging to a responsible breeder. These dogs can be just as healthy as larger ones, but consider it a red flag when the terms teacup, pocket-sized, miniature, or tiny-toy are used to describe a dog, as no formal size differentiation exists. Chihuahuas only come in two varieties—long and smooth coat; there are no other types.

Dogs that fall between 4 and 6 pounds (1.8 and 2.7 kg) are best if you plan to show your Chihuahua or compete in any organised activities. Chihuahuas weighing less than 4 pounds are not recommended for inexperienced dog owners.

DEER TYPE

You may have also heard of another kind of Chihuahua referred to as the deer type. While far less harmful than the teacup misnomer, this is also an owner-invented term. Resembling deer fawns, these Chihuahuas have longer legs, more slender builds, and longer snouts than that of dogs fitting the breed's standard. There are usually no health risks associated with this unofficial type, but beware of any seller attempting to claim or charge for something they're not.

IS THE CHIHUAHUA RIGHT FOR YOU?

Although the breed standard is fundamental in maintaining the integrity of each unique breed, it is wise to remember that a standard describes an ideal dog. Rarely is there even a champion that possesses all the specific qualities of his breed's standard. If you don't plan on showing your Chihuahua, such criteria may still be useful for selecting a well-rounded puppy, but keep in mind that even dogs with overshot bites or thin coats can make excellent pets. By searching for the perfect dog, aesthetically speaking, you may miss the Chihuahua that is perfect for you!

Show-quality or Pet-quality?

If you wish to purchase a show dog, expect to pay more for him than for a pet-quality dog. You should also be prepared for a longer wait. Oftentimes breeders like to keep show-quality dogs for future breeding. These dogs possess all the best characteristics relating to both health and temperament that help produce strong and friendly puppies.

If you think in terms of paying by the pound, Chihuahuas may seem expensive. While you may pay more for a quality purebred Chihuahua than some other breeds, a moderately higher price is often understandable. Because a Chihuahua puppy's head is so large in proportion to his body, natural deliveries can be extremely

What Is a Breed Standard?

For each breed eligible for AKC or KC registration, there is an official breed standard. This description of an ideal dog is used as a guideline for the judging of conformation events. It also serves as a model for breeders. Although the standard describes the perfect dog, very rarely does such a faultless dog exist. The full breed standard can be found on the Kennel Club website (www.thekennelclub.org.uk).

difficult and dangerous for both mother and pups. Caesarean sections are often warranted, adding to the breeder's costs significantly.

Do your homework, and beware of dogs bearing unusually low upfront price tags, as an unhealthy dog will ultimately cost you dearly, both monetarily and emotionally. If money is a major concern, please consider adoption or rescue. Many wonderful homeless Chihuahuas throughout the country are waiting for devoted owners just like you.

Whichever route you decide on, the most important thing is that you are sure of the dog you choose. Chihuahuas have one of the longest life spans of all dog breeds. With our increasing knowledge in such areas as canine nutrition and medical care, many Chihuahuas are living well into their teens. Every dog deserves an equally long-lived home in which he will be responsibly cared for and loved.

The Chihuahua Temperament: Aptitude for Attitude

Best known for being the world's smallest dog, the Chihuahua is anything but light on personality. Like other toy breeds, the

Chihuahuas live longer than most other dog breeds.

Chihuahua's primary role is companionship, but don't confuse his desire for affection with a docile nature. Words commonly used to describe this breed include lively, courageous, and saucy.

Because of their high energy levels and playful temperaments, Chihuahuas are often likened to terriers. Also similar to many terriers, Chihuahuas possess little understanding of their size. This brave little dog is surprisingly quick to defend both home and family. His watchdog tendencies may be rooted more in bravado than brawn, but it can be a heartwarming guise of protection nonetheless.

A Dog of Many

Although the Chihuahua comes in all colours, the most common are fawn, brindle fawn, chocolate, white, cream, silver fawn, black and tan, and black.

Long or Short Coat?

Although some owners and breeders claim that under their fur long and smooth coat Chihuahuas are identical, many insist there is a notable personality difference between the two varieties. The smooth coats have a reputation for being a bit bolder in temperament, whereas long coats are often said to be a bit more reserved, yet playful.

Once you decide this breed is right for you, your next decision will be which variety you prefer. Whether or not you notice a difference in personality, there are a few contrasts between the long and smooth coats on which most agree.

Both types are very content lap dogs, but smooth coats are more liable to sit in your lap, whereas long coats are more apt to sit beside you. Sitting directly in his owner's lap for long periods of time can raise a long-coat Chihuahua's body temperature to the point of panting. For similar reasons, long coats prefer to lie on top of the bed covers instead of under them, where you will more often find a smooth coat.

All Chihuahuas are sensitive to cold temperatures, but owners need to use extra care with smooth coats, especially those lacking undercoats. Long coats can withstand low temperatures longer than their shorter-haired counterparts, but it is a wise idea to dress either in a sweater for outdoor time during cold weather. Since the average Chihuahua stands just 6 to 9 inches tall (15.2 to 22.9 cm), use caution when taking your dog outside in the snow. To a Chihuahua, walking in just 3 inches (7.6 cm) of snow is comparable to a human's having to trudge through 2 feet (.6 m) or more. Also, if your Chihuahua gets wet, be sure to dry the dog thoroughly once back indoors.

Chihuahuas can easily acclimate to either city or country living.

Finally, you may notice that longhaired Chihuahuas shed less than shorthaired dogs. Neither sheds a considerable volume, but long coats tend to shed seasonally, while smooth coats seem to be trapped in a continuous shedding cycle. You will need to spend a bit more time grooming a long coat, however, so there are pros and cons to both varieties.

Chihuahua Behaviour

Chihuahuas bond extremely closely with their owners and tend to seek out one person in particular whom they prefer to all others. Their loyalty is unsurpassed, with a strong tendency for possessiveness. They need to be trained gently, but never halfheartedly.

The Chihuahua is a clever, independent breed that responds well to consistent training when initiated early by the owner. A Chihuahua must learn the word "no", or anarchy may result. If you assume that such a petite lovable puppy doesn't need training, you might soon find that your perceptive little dog has instead trained you. More than one unruly Chihuahua has been aptly named Napoleon.

Although many Chihuahuas seem fearless, some dogs may shiver violently when scared, excited, or cold. If you notice your dog shaking, first make sure he is warm. If there is no obvious cause for fear or excitement, the shaking may be related to a high metabolism, but it is a good idea to have your vet check the animal to confirm this is the case.

Male or Female?

Just as some owners prefer long coats to smooth coats (and vice versa), many people will select a male or female Chihuahua based on gender alone. Frequently this partiality is linked to a formerly cherished pet of the same sex, and the preference can be deeply ingrained. Each dog is unique, of course, but similar to human genetics, there are differences that appear to go along with either an x or y canine chromosome.

As someone who has owned male dogs, I must confess that I think the boys sometimes get a bad rap. Male dogs are often labelled more aggressive, harder to housetrain, and more destructive than females. Is all of this true? Much depends on the individual dog. In my experience I have found males equally loving as females, just as quick (or slow—again, depending on the dog) to housetrain, and unfortunately, yes, oftentimes a bit more destructive. I have also found them to be less moody and more tolerant of children.

Unneutered males can be a different story. When a male dog's reproductive system is left intact, that dog is more likely to act aggressively when he reaches sexual maturity due to the increased level of testosterone. There are many health advantages to spaying or neutering your Chihuahua, but for a male dog many of the benefits are temperamental. Neutered males are easier to train, more tolerant of other male dogs, and far less prone to annoying behaviours like urine marking.

I have also owned female dogs and certainly understand why so many dog lovers adore little girls so much. Females are said to be less distractible during training, less brazen about demanding their owners' attention, and subtler in their defiance—and these are

Chihuahuas may bond to one person more closely than they do to anyone else.

No Roughhousing!

Avoid games that pit your strength against your Chihuahua's. Tug-of-war may help you direct your dog's attention to an acceptable chewing item, but it can also encourage aggression.

usually accurate assertions. Females tend to be less aggressive with their owners, but they are just as (if not more) domineering with other dogs, particularly other females. They are also by and large craftier about their stubbornness.

A common myth about females is that a dog should have at least one litter before being spayed. Many people mistakenly believe that motherhood makes a dog a better pet. The truth is that giving birth and raising puppies does not affect a female dog's personality. Pet overpopulation is a critical problem in this country; no dog should ever be bred for the futile purpose of improving her temperament this way.

Many people also wrongly assume that male dogs are the only ones to act out sexually, using a toy or a human's leg, for instance, as an object of immediate gratification. Countless owners report that females perform this act, as well. Early spaying and neutering is the best way to help reduce incidences of a sexual nature, but the fact is this behaviour isn't always rooted in sexuality. Often it is actually an act of dominance—a dog's way of trying to exert authority.

The best thing to do when comparing the sexes is to evaluate your household's present circumstances—and even your own personality. There is nothing wrong about preferring one gender to the other. One may indeed be a better choice for you and your family, but both males and females make wonderful pets—eager to love and be loved.

At Home in Town or Country

While some dogs are better suited for the town or the country, the Chihuahua is one breed that can easily acclimate to either environment. These dogs are remarkably portable. They can be carried virtually anywhere, but they also revel in walking on a lead. Like other dog breeds, a Chihuahua should never be allowed to run free without a proper fence or other enclosure, but one certainly doesn't need acres of land for this breed to have an adequate garden for play and exercise. A small flat or apartment in town can easily serve as a playground for this adaptable pet.

Many Chihuahuas thrive in a flat setting, with staircases and limited space posing little difficulty to most dogs and owners. One thing that flat dwellers must consider, however, is noise. While you may view your dog as outgoing and quick to express his opinions,

Exercise Precautions

- Keep a close eye on your dog: watch for any unusual signs of fatigue or trouble breathing. If your pup wants to stop, let him. Dogs that overdo it can suffer strained tendons or ligaments or other orthopaedic problems.
- Don't expect your fuzzy buddy to be a weekend warrior, even if you only get exercise on the weekends yourself. After a long week without exercise, your dog may be ready to get out and burn off energy. But because of their enthusiasm, many dogs will overdo it.
- Safety first—keep your Chihuahua on a lead. Even the best-trained dogs can run into the path of a car or a territorial animal. And if you have to go when it's dark out, put reflectors on your dog's collar as well as on your clothes.
- Concrete and asphalt are tough on the paws, especially on hot days. Try to walk on dirt paths or grass as much as possible. Gravel, cinders, and road salt can also irritate paws.
- Take it easy in extreme weather. If it's freezing cold or hot and steamy out, either keep your walk short or play a little indoor fetch instead.
- The more active your dog is, the more water he'll need. Make sure he has plenty of fresh water before and after your walk. If you're going for a long walk, take some water along for him.
  (Courtesy of the American Animal Hospital Association.)

a neighbour with thin walls may describe your Chihuahua as yappy. Chihuahuas possess an especially keen sense of hearing and are often the first to alert you to a visitor's arrival—or any other questionable sound.

Extreme caution is needed for outdoor areas where other animals might come into contact with your dog. A neighbour's perfectly friendly collie could fatally wound your Chihuahua in just seconds by simply trying to initiate play. Seldom aware of their strength, larger dogs can easily step on a Chihuahua or grab him and break his neck with one quick shake.

Indoors or Outdoors?

Chihuahuas are generally not outdoor dogs. Although they enjoy taking leisurely walks with their owners and romping outside on sunny days, they typically prefer cuddles to hikes—and whether seeking love or warmth, often prefer to be touching you. Chihuahuas are extremely vulnerable to cold weather, their size and close proximity to the ground making it difficult for their bodies to retain heat. Many understandably detest rain and other harsh elements.

Speaking of harsh elements, remember that the sun can be the harshest of all. Dogs with fair skin, short hair, and light-coloured coats are all especially susceptible to sunburn, but any dog can burn if exposed to the sun for too long. Any body part not covered by fur—primarily the nose, tips of ears, and belly—also can be particularly vulnerable.

The best protection is staying out of direct sunlight during the middle of the day. If your dog is going to be out and about on a sunny day, make sure to use sunscreen. Canine versions of this human must-have item are designed specifically for your dog's skin and can be purchased from a number of pet supply retailers.

You can also use your own sunscreen in a pinch. Just use the same rules you do for human use—go with a sun protection factor (SPF) of at least 15 and make sure your product is PABA-free. PABA (para-aminobenzoic acid), a chemical that absorbs ultraviolet (UV) light, is dangerous for dogs if licked or ingested. Zinc oxide, a common ingredient in human sunscreens and a popular product on its own, is similarly toxic to dogs—so read those labels carefully!

It may be inevitable that your Chihuahua will lick off some of the product. An excellent diversionary tactic is offering a dog biscuit or other favourite food item immediately after application. The Chihuahua may forget about the sunscreen when presented with the treat.

Keep an eye on your Chihuahuas when they are outside—the sun can burn their delicate skin.

Time Needs

Although this breed is highly adaptable, one thing to which a Chihuahua should not have to adjust is being alone for regular extended periods of time. Does this mean you are not a suitable Chihuahua owner if you work? Certainly not. For most people work is a necessary part of life. People tend to work longer hours these days, and yet more and more households include dogs. Although the most common, work isn't the only reason we have for not being home much. Our busy lives may be filled with everything from the respites of dining out and taking in movies to the mundane business of running errands. Whether it's work or personal, however, leaving a Chihuahua alone at length too frequently is neither fair nor practical.

Some breeds might tolerate being left to fend for themselves relatively well, but the Chihuahua is not one of them. If left alone too long repeatedly, a Chihuahua will likely experience separation anxiety, a problem that can manifest itself in any number of unpleasant ways, including excessive barking and howling, destructive chewing, and even soiling of the house.

One way to minimise these behaviours is providing your Chihuahua with a special toy before you leave—preferably one that you have rubbed with your hands, infusing the item with your scent. Be sure to say goodbye, as this can help build your dog's comfort and confidence, but refrain from prolonging the process. This will only increase your dog's anxiety about your imminent departure.

Preventing the problem entirely is best by making sure your Chihuahua is alone for long periods of time as seldom as possible.

Rules for Children and Chihuahuas

Above and beyond the universal rules for the interaction of dogs and children, there are some special things to consider when the dog is a Chihuahua:

- Never leave a child with a Chihuahua unsupervised—ever.
- The most important word to teach your child is gentle, gentle, gentle! The child must understand that no matter how cute they are, Chihuahuas are not toys.
- Only allow a child to hold your dog when the child is sitting firmly on the floor. (The sofa doesn't count!) Under no circumstance should the dog be picked up or carried by a child.
- Teach your child to stay out of the Chihuahua's face. This is a good rule with any dog, but a closely approaching child can easily frighten a small dog, and frightened dogs tend to snap or bite in order to protect themselves.
- Look before you sit! This is a good rule for all family members, but children may need extra reminding, as Chihuahuas can easily hide behind pillows, stuffed animals—virtually anything.
- Keep food at the table. While parents often encourage their children to share, this is one time when it can be a bad thing. Many human treats like chocolate, which is toxic to all dogs, are especially dangerous for smaller breeds. To avoid the possibility of accidental poisoning, keep all food where you can supervise its consumption.
- Whenever appropriate, involve your child with the care of your Chihuahua. Teaching your child about brushing, feeding, and walking your dog—as well as gentle play—will also teach your Chihuahua that children can be enjoyable companions.

A good rule is to never leave your dog alone for more than four hours without giving him a chance to relieve himself. Small dogs have small bladders!

One strategy for making sure your Chihuahua is receiving adequate attention, even if you are away from home most of the day, is to spend some time together before you leave. Setting your alarm just fifteen minutes early can provide the two of you with enough opportunity for a short walk or a rousing indoor play session each morning. Dogs love to nap after energetic activities, and what better time for this nonactivity than when you need to be elsewhere?

In addition to providing your Chihuahua with regular walks for the purpose of toileting, try to give your dog a recreational outing at least once a week. It doesn't have to be a big production. Just getting out to the park or the pet shop (outside his normal four walls) will help ease the monotony of being a housedog for five or more days a week. Whether visiting a friend or returning a film to the video shop, allowing your Chihuahua to simply tag along is a fun way to show your dog how much you value his company. For your dog's safety, though, please never leave your Chihuahua unattended in your vehicle.

Your Chihuahua may be easy to carry, but don't just tote him everywhere and neglect his exercise needs.

Exercise Needs

Chihuahuas relish activity. You can easily fulfil your dog's exercise needs by simply including him in your own daily routine. If you enjoy walking, take daily jaunts together. If you prefer an indoor setting, consider games that include playing with your Chihuahua's favourite toy. Well-liked canine games include hide-and-seek and fetch, but you and your dog can even make up your own. Puppies are especially adept at play—the most efficient form of canine exercise.

Chihuahuas also enjoy more ceremonial forms of exercise, such as competing in obedience and agility. Although the dogs on the heavier end of the breed's weight range are usually better suited to these activities, Chihuahuas of all sizes may compete in these events. Of course, competitions are optional. A good friend of mine practices agility with her dogs, but elects not to participate in formal matches. She prefers working with her dogs at home just for fun, and the dogs really seem to enjoy the activity, as well.

Regardless of what kind of exercise you prefer, it is vital that your dog is provided with some time each day for keeping fit. Because Chihuahuas are so light, it is easy to carry them around almost everywhere. One disadvantage to doing so is that they often miss out on much needed exercise. Exercising your Chihuahua is one of the best ways to help keep him fit and healthy. These little dogs have hearty appetites and can quickly become overweight if their need for exercise is unfulfilled.

Many Chihuahuas become destructive if not given a sufficient amount of exercise. Your dog is far less likely to take his pent up energy out on your new leather shoes if he is getting regular walks or play sessions. Exercise also helps maintain canine health, since obesity is a major contributor to such problems as heart disease, arthritis, and diabetes.

You may be wondering if there are any physical limitations for this breed due to his diminutive size. Those who know Chihuahuas best have learned that there is little this breed cannot do. Still one must consider the size and normal activity level of any animal before beginning a new exercise routine.

If your dog is new to regular exercise, start with short walks and gradually increase the time to a total that appears comfortable for your dog. Also, remember when you are walking together that your Chihuahua needs to take several steps for every one of yours.

Chihuahuas can get along with other dogs if socialised properly.

You can give your dog quite a workout without breaking a sweat yourself.

Chihuahuas and Children

When deciding if the Chihuahua is right for you, you should also consider whether you and your family are right for this breed. If you have small children, the answer is likely no. The problem is not that Chihuahuas are bad with children. When treated with proper respect, the Chihuahua will integrate into a family with children quite well. It only takes one overly harsh squeeze by a fascinated little boy or girl, however, for your dog—and possibly your child—to become seriously injured.

A parent needs to exercise extreme caution when allowing interaction between a child and any animal. Being so exceptionally small, the Chihuahua is particularly vulnerable to the erratic (albeit innocent) actions of a toddler, preschooler, or any small child. Young children, even the best behaved, often lose their balance, throw tantrums, and playfully roughhouse. Any one of these habits could prove disastrous with a 4-pound (1.8 kg) dog in the house. Young children also have a tendency to move very quickly, leaving a Chihuahua unsure of the child's intent, and inadvertently causing the dog to react aggressively.

This doesn't mean that if you are a parent you must rule out the breed; you simply need to make sure the timing is right before introducing a Chihuahua into your home. Older children can easily learn appropriate ways of interacting with this breed. With constant vigilance and dedication to teaching the right habits early, you might find that even somewhat younger children can live peaceably alongside Chihuahuas. I know one owner, now a retired AKC judge, who successfully raised four children alongside her first Chihuahua.

Small Dogs and Small Children

Younger children need to be very closely supervised around all dogs, but especially smaller breeds such as the Chihuahua, as a child can accidentally hurt a dog while playing, or even make him react aggressively to quick, erratic movements.

Perhaps the children you need to consider are not your own. Once a Chihuahua is part of your household, every child (or adult) that enters your home needs to understand the same rules. Even if you think the rules are obvious, they might not be so evident to a child or an adult without Chihuahua experience. Your dog depends on you to make his needs clear.

Remember, your Chihuahua may be just as protective of you as you are of him. While they love their family members to a fault, Chihuahuas are generally suspicious of strangers and might be downright sassy to them. Socialisation helps, of course, but a mere tolerance of strangers might be the best you can expect from your Chihuahua.

For everyone's protection you may need to put your dog in his crate or in another room when unexpected company arrives, especially those with boisterous children. One Chihuahua owner I know has found that placing her dog in a playpen in her bedroom works very well for this purpose.

Interaction With Other Pets

A fellow canine companion is quite possibly the best gift an owner can give his or her dog. More than one book has been written on the very subject of how dogs crave one another's company. Extreme care needs to be used, however, when adding this quintessential cohort to your family—even more care than you used when selecting your first dog. You must consider the breed, age, temperament, and history of this new dog—and be certain that it will be a safe mix.

Chihuahuas typically love other Chihuahuas. What is more impressive, though, is how they always seem to know their own kind. Often referred to as clannish, most Chihuahuas prefer their own breed to others.

It is tempting to assume that the more Chihuahuas may be merrier. After all, with their diminutive stature, these dogs don't eat much compared to other breeds, and they require very little space.

It is important to realise, though, that the company of other animals cannot take the place of having a dedicated human master. An owner must have sufficient time for each and every dog in the household.

Chihuahuas' needs for love and attention not only equal, but often exceed that of other breeds. Feeding multiple Chihuahuas may not break your budget, but adding just one dog also means doubling the amount of time you spend doing things like training, grooming, and cleaning up. It will also double your veterinary bills.

One of the biggest factors in a Chihuahua's positive interactions with other breeds and pets of other species is whether or not the dog was raised with these animals. Chihuahuas do have a reputation for disliking other dog breeds, but this isn't always the case. They can actually be quite accepting of other dogs when socialised properly. Even if belligerent to the dog next door, a Chihuahua will most likely get along with—or at the very least ignore—another pet within his own household.

One breeder told me that she has had a Labrador Retriever, cats, and even horses over the years with her Chihuahuas. "In fact," she confided to me, "the barn cats used to nurse the Chihuahuas. The dogs acted like the ice cream truck just pulled up. The Chihuahuas of all ages would do it, and the cats seemed to stay in milk all year."

Chihuahuas typically love other Chihuahuas—they have a knack for knowing their own kind.

Introducing an extremely large dog into your Chihuahua's household could surely spell trouble, whether the two get along or not. Dogs get along best when they are allowed to establish their own hierarchy, but with an imposing size difference you may be hard pressed to allow this natural order to fall into place. Just one serious confrontation—possibly even initiated by your Chihuahua—could be deadly.

One last thing to consider

Make sure your child understands how to be gentle with the family Chihuahua.

when adding a second pet to your household is the gender of your current pet. If you already own a Chihuahua, how does he get along with animals of the same sex? The opposite sex? Many veterinarians and other experts recommend either a male/male or male/female combination. Female dogs will sometimes establish an unending rivalry for the position of top dog. This competition may be harmless, but it can also be dangerous if taken too far.

C h a p t e r

3

PREPARING

for Your Chihuahua

Now that you have decided that the Chihuahua is the perfect dog to join your family, you need to do some research and preparation. First, take some time to decide if a puppy or an adult is right for you, then locate the best place to obtain your Chihuahua, and finally prepare your home for your new arrival.

PUPPY OR ADULT?

Is there anything cuter than a Chihuahua puppy? For many of us the idea of getting a dog instantly inspires an image of a teeny being, just weeks old, and taking him home with us to begin his new life. He depends on us, and we want to give him all the love and attention we can. The great thing about a Chihuahua is that he doesn't necessarily have to be a puppy for you to enjoy this scenario. Unlike a larger breed (such as a Saint Bernard or Newfoundland), a Chihuahua will still be small whether he is five months old or five years old, and an older homeless dog may need you even more than a younger one.

Making the decision between acquiring a puppy or an adult dog is an easy one for many, but if you find yourself torn between the two, consider your circumstances. There are definite advantages to both choices, often depending on your lifestyle.

Younger Chihuahuas arrive with far less history. This can be an advantage if you have children or pets already in the household. Younger dogs are also far less likely to possess deeply ingrained behaviours that need correcting, a benefit for someone with limited time.

In contrast, most adult dogs are already housebroken and possess an established personality. They will generally require far less training and supervision than a brand-new pup. If you yourself are older, the demands of an overly energetic puppy might be more taxing than you would prefer.

Many people are naturally drawn to puppies, and owning a dog for his entire lifetime is very appealing, but since Chihuahuas are so long lived, this is far less an issue for this breed

'Tis Not the Season

The holidays might seem like the perfect time to welcome a Chihuahua into your family. Countless films and television programmes have created an enduring image of an adorable puppy wrapped with a festive red ribbon, making the whole family glow with delight on Christmas morning. While the story seems pleasing, the reality is that a dog should never be given as a gift.

Even if your idea is to adopt or buy a Chihuahua for yourself, it is a good idea to hold off until after the holidays. Impulse decisions come easy at this time; it is far too simple to get caught up in the spirit of the season. Maybe a Chihuahua puppy looks so cute, you just have to have him to spend the holidays with you. Perhaps you think buying him for your grandmother would make it so that she did not have to be alone for the holidays. Perhaps you have always wanted a Chihuahua yourself and think that you deserve a special present this year. Or maybe your son or daughter wants a puppy more than anything in the world. Unfortunately, none of these reasons alone is the right one for getting a dog.

Bringing a dog into your household is a serious commitment of time and money, one that needs to be discussed with everyone within the household in which the dog will live. A dog should never be a surprise gift. Maybe Grandma would prefer not to have to clean up after a dog because of her aching back. Perhaps you haven't gotten that Chihuahua you've always wanted because you really don't have time for him. And maybe your son or daughter isn't quite old enough for a Chihuahua, or any dog, just yet.

If charity is your goal, there are numerous canine organisations that can always use a helping hand during the holidays, as well as any other time of the year, but the best thing you can do for any dog is wait until those holiday bells stop ringing.

than others. Shelters are full of dogs in every age group—from puppies not yet old enough for adoption to seniors. There really is no ideal age for a Chihuahua; it's all a matter of matching the right dog with his best owner.

THE SEARCH FOR THE CHIHUAHUA OF YOUR DREAMS

Whether you decide on a puppy or an adult dog, a reputable breeder is one of the best resources for finding the Chihuahua that's right for you. Locating a quality breeder isn't difficult, but it may take a little time. The national kennel clubs have excellent websites that include various kinds of referral links—from national and local breed clubs, breed rescues, and even classifieds. You can also attend national events to meet people involved with the breed, or ask a veterinarian familiar with Chihuahuas to recommend a trusted breeder. These are all constructive starting points.

Attending dog shows is a wonderful way to meet breeders and other Chihuahua enthusiasts. You might not want to initiate a conversation while the owners are preparing their dogs for competition, but you may be able to approach one once his or her dog's turn in the ring is over. Most breeders and handlers take great pleasure in answering questions about their favourite subject—Chihuahuas.

Types of Breeders

Just as with any business, there are responsible and irresponsible people involved in the breeding of dogs. Many of the best breeders cannot be found in your local yellow pages. A good number don't even advertise their pups, but instead prefer to keep waiting lists for upcoming litters. These are often referred to as hobby breeders. A hobby breeder's dogs might be show dogs, but they are also pets, and their kennel is the breeder's home. Since they don't depend on breeding for income, hobby breeders have the freedom to focus on bettering the breed, not just selling dogs. A hobby breeder will usually offer just one breed, two at the most. They often have just one or two litters per year, so you may need to be patient for a pup. If you want a dog sooner, most hobby breeders can recommend a Chihuahua rescue group in your area.

Hobby breeders are among the most responsible in their field. Chihuahuas produced by most hobby breeders are well worth the wait for a puppy. Since they are bred from carefully selected parents and raised in loving homes, these puppies usually have excellent temperaments.

One other type of breeder you may encounter is a backyard breeder. These are most often owners who decided to start breeding pets for fun. Even though they may love their dogs very much, breeding without doing thorough research can be irresponsible. Also, dogs sold by backyard breeders are unlikely to come with any sort of guarantee or follow-up.

What to Look for in a Breeder

Do your homework first, so you know beforehand which questions will be most relevant. Ask as many questions as you can, and be prepared to answer some, as well. Good breeders

How to Identify a Good Breeder

Look for a breeder who at minimum:
- Has dogs that appear happy and healthy, are excited to meet new people, and don't shy away from visitors.
- Shows you where the dogs spend most of their time—an area that is clean and well maintained.
- Encourages you to spend time with the puppy's parents (or at a least the pup's mother) when you visit.
- Breeds only one or two types of dogs and is knowledgeable about breed standards.
- Has a strong relationship with a local veterinarian and shows you records of veterinary visits for the puppies; explains the puppy's medical history and what vaccinations your new puppy will need.
- Is well versed in the potential genetic problems inherent to the breed (there are specific genetic concerns for every breed) and explains to you what those concerns are. The breeder should have had the puppy's parents tested (and should have the results for the parents' parents) to ensure they are free of those defects. She should be able to provide you with documentation for all testing she has done.
- Gives you guidance on caring and training for your puppy and is available for assistance after you take your puppy home.
- Provides references of other families who have purchased puppies from him or her.
- Feeds high-quality, premium-brand dog food.
- Doesn't always have puppies available, but rather will keep a list of interested people for his or her next available litter.
- Encourages multiple visits and wants your entire family to meet the puppy before you take your puppy home.
- Provides you with a written contract and health guarantee and allows plenty of time for you to read it thoroughly. The breeder should not require that you use a specific veterinarian.

will ask you just as many questions, if not more, than you ask them.

While memberships in organisations such as breed clubs are a definite advantage, you must not assume that these affiliations alone equal a trustworthy breeder. Good breeders are involved with the breed to produce healthy, good-tempered dogs that fit the Chihuahua breed standard as closely as possible. Beware of any breeder who only wishes to discuss money.

The first meeting should go a bit like an adoption interview. The breeder will likely ask you many questions, carefully screening you as a potential owner for one of his or her puppies. Don't be offended by this, as you should both be acting in the best interest of the dog. You may be asked such things as why you want a Chihuahua, what other animals you already own, and who else will be living with and caring for the new puppy. You may also be asked to bring proof from your landlord that owning a dog is allowed if you rent a flat. You will also be able to ask your own questions of the breeder.

Many breeders often only have one or two litters of puppies available per year. This ensures the health of both mom and her babies.

Once You've Found Your Breeder

If you both decide that one of the Chihuahua puppies is right for you, the next step will be the paperwork. Most breeders of this kind require a buyer to sign a written agreement. This document will clearly outline the responsibilities of both owner and breeder. Usually it states that the breeder will take the dog back at any time for any reason—and that you must consult the breeder if you ever find yourself unable to care for the animal. Many agreements will include a clause, specifying that the breeder must approve any new home, and that he or she will take the animal if no suitable home exists. Good breeders don't want their dogs ending up in shelters or unfit homes. You will also agree to have your Chihuahua spayed or neutered once he or she is old enough—or after you are done showing the animal, if you purchased a show dog.

A good breeder will provide you with your dog's pedigree and health records when you first acquire him.

The breeder should provide you with a pedigree, showing you appropriate health clearances for both sire and dam and the puppy's ancestors. Bloodlines and inheritable traits should be explained to you at this time. The breeder should provide a written

How to Register Your Dog With the KC

In Britain, the Kennel Club offers a "Guide to Litter Registration Booklet" for information. Registering a puppy begins with the breeder, who requests to register the litter using a "Form One". The breeder sends "Form One" and the requested fee to the KC. The KC then sends the breeder a Litter Registration Certifiate and one Breeder Registration Certificate for each puppy in the litter.

When the breeder sells the puppy, the breeder signs and completes the "date of sale" part on the back of the Breeder Registration Certificate. This certificate is then given to the puppy owner. The owner must complete the Change of Ownership form and send it to the KC within 10 days. The KC then sends the new owner a Registration Certificate. Health insurance for registered dogs is also available.

guarantee for the health of the Chihuahua.

You should also be given the puppy's immunisation record and schedule. Many breeders will send you home with detailed feeding instructions for the first few weeks, as well as the name of a trusted veterinarian. You should also be given paperwork to transfer ownership of your new Chihuahua with the KC.

If your puppy isn't yet ready to go home, consider bringing a small soft toy to leave with him after you go. You may want to sleep with the item the night before your visit, so it is sure to be infused with your scent. Because dogs rely so heavily on scent, this can help familiarise your puppy with his new owner and home weeks before he arrives.

If you haven't decided what to call your new Chihuahua, start thinking about it now. Baby name books can be a wonderful resource for selecting the name that best suits your dog. Many owners choose Mexican names for their Chihuahuas, but the choices are limitless. Let your breeder know as soon as you have chosen the name, so your puppy can start learning his right away.

If you are not able to locate a breeder in your area, you might consider purchasing a puppy from a breeder in another part of the country. There are many wonderful Chihuahua breeders throughout the UK, but even more caution needs to be used when going the long-distance route. If you are unable to travel to the breeder yourself, do you know anyone who does live close enough for a visit? This person should be someone you trust and have armed with information about evaluating the dogs' environment. He or she can even bring along a video camera and record the meeting for you. Ask for references from the breeder, and follow up by contacting them.

Breeders sometimes bring in dogs from overseas in order to introduce a new bloodline. Shipping is probably the biggest downfall to buying a dog in this manner. You will be responsible for the cost of shipping, along with your Chihuahua's crate—an item that can be extremely useful in the housetraining process after your dog arrives, so consider this expenditure an investment. Tell the breeder you would prefer a direct flight on a weekday, so you can hopefully avoid a busy time at the airport. The breeder should provide you with the flight number, time of arrival, and airway bill number for your arriving Chihuahua.

Expect the puppy to be exhausted after his long journey. Bring along your dog's lead and harness, so you can provide him with a chance to relieve himself as soon as possible. You may also want to postpone a more animated greeting until you and your new puppy arrive home.

Adoption Options

Adoption can be the easiest and most inexpensive way of finding a Chihuahua that needs you just as much as you want a Chihuahua. Many of these dogs have lost their homes due to changes in their previous owners' lives (such as new babies, divorces, or moving), not because there is anything wrong with the dogs. This doesn't mean that you won't have to spend some time looking for your Chihuahua, but it does make adoption a realistic option for someone who has already settled on this specific breed.

Contacting your nearest Chihuahua rescue group is one of the best ways to find a dog in need of a new home. Not only can these organisations usually point you toward a Chihuahua faster than an animal shelter, but the people involved are also armed with breed-specific knowledge that can be especially helpful after the adoption process. Your veterinarian, breeder, or local animal shelter can refer you to a Chihuahua rescue organisation in your area.

Once you find a rescue group, ask as many questions as you can. Whenever possible you should know the dog's age and background. How are the Chihuahuas cared for prior to adoption? What criteria are used for determining which dogs are candidates for placement? Have the foster owners noticed any behaviour problems that might be an issue? Does the rescue group offer any post-adoption services, such as training or referrals?

A Chihuahua adopted from an animal shelter can be every bit as good a pet as one found through a rescue group. If you are lucky enough to find a Chihuahua at one of these facilities, you should follow the same guidelines as with a rescue group. As a prospective adoptive owner, you should be just as thorough in your selection process as a prospective buyer would be in searching for the right dog. Your biggest responsibility in either case is providing the Chihuahua you choose with a lifelong home.

A Chihuahua adopted from an animal shelter or a rescue can make a great pet.

PUPPY-PROOFING YOUR HOME

Before introducing your Chihuahua to his new home, you must first take a few steps to ensure the safety of your new pet. Some of the necessary tasks of puppy-proofing a house or flat are quite similar to those of expectant parents preparing their home for a baby's arrival. Like babies, young Chihuahuas are extraordinarily curious about the world around them, but they cannot discern an item of enjoyment from one of danger. For safety's sake, you might want to pick up a baby gate. This item will come in handy for keeping your dog in a room that has been completely puppy-proofed whenever you need to be elsewhere.

The best time to begin preparations for your dog's arrival is well

Try to limit activity for your Chihuahua on his homecoming day until he's had all of his shots and is comfortable in his new home.

in advance of homecoming day. If you and other family members are currently in the habit of kicking off your shoes when you get home and leaving them by the door, this is the time for a new routine. Shoe leather can be especially useful for easing the pain of puppy teething, but a Nylabone is a less expensive and more appropriate teething toy.

Small Objects

Like young children, puppies seem to predictably put everything into their mouths. Your Chihuahua puppy can swallow any small object left in his path, and many substances can cause serious injury, or even death.

Dangers lurk everywhere—from the contents of your rubbish bin to items you might never imagine would interest your dog. Paper clips, elastics, coins, even jewellery can choke your Chihuahua or end up in his digestive tract, and unless they pass completely through, your dog will need costly surgery to remove them. Keep wastebaskets behind closed doors or out of reach until you get a sense of your dog's tendencies. It is a good idea to place any particularly dangerous items in an outdoor rubbish bin almost immediately. A dull razor that you or your spouse tossed away this morning could hurt your Chihuahua disastrously this afternoon.

Blinds

Many of the same items that threaten human toddlers also pose a threat to your Chihuahua. If your home is among the many with Venetian blinds, be sure that the cords are tied securely out of reach of your dog. Just as the far too many children who have been strangled with these outer cords, your Chihuahua could fall victim to a similarly tragic accident. Also, beware of the inner cord that runs throughout the blind slats. Many people don't realise that this part of the blind can also strangle a child or small animal.

Electrical Cables and Outlets

Make sure all electric cables are inaccessible to your Chihuahua. You may have to bundle long cables or tie them out of reach. Any unused electrical outlets should be covered. Use the individual plastic shields found in the baby section of any department store.

Chihuahua puppies are remarkably quick little beings. You might think the only times for concern are those when you leave the room, but your pup can often grab any forbidden item that tempts him while you avert your eyes for mere seconds. You cannot rely on even the most careful supervision for keeping your dog safe; you must remove the dangers from his reach.

Plants

Some of the most common household dangers for dogs are plants. It is best to elevate all your plants well out of your dog's reach. (Remember, this means your dog shouldn't have access to them from any furniture item on which he is allowed to sit.) Even certain vegetable plants can be toxic to dogs. For example, the vines of tomato and spinach plants can make your dog sick—and even prove fatal in some instances.

Medications

Human medications can also be highly toxic to dogs. Never give your dog any human medication unless prescribed by your veterinarian. Common human painkillers such as acetaminophen, ibuprofen, and aspirin can be deadly to dogs—as can

Common Household Dangers to Your Chihuahua

CHEMICALS	FOODS	PLANTS	OTHER ITEMS
Antifreeze	Alcoholic or caffeinated beverages	Azalea	Craft items
Fertilizers		Geranium	Dental floss
Plant foods	Chocolate	Mistletoe	Sponges
Household cleaners	Onions	Oleander	Tinsel
Moth balls	Grapes and raisins	Philodendron	Toys with removable parts (such as eyes)
Potpourri oils	Yeast dough	Poinsettia	

Remember, this is just a partial list. Ask your veterinarian for a more complete list of items that can be toxic to your dog. Treat your Chihuahua like you would an infant, keeping all chemicals and potential choking hazards out of reach. If you are unsure if a particular food is safe for your dog, don't offer it.

antidepressants, diet pills, and vitamins.

Get On Your Chihuahua's Level

Finally, when you think you have covered all the bases, put yourself in your dog's position—literally. Getting down on the floor and looking at a room from your Chihuahua's perspective can reveal many things you may have missed, from any uncovered electrical outlets to items accidentally left under furniture. Unless you look for it, you might never notice that exposed nail on the underside of your sofa, but your Chihuahua could suffer a serious laceration by unknowingly crawling past it when his ball rolls under the couch.

Most dangerous items remain a threat regardless of your Chihuahua's age. Many dogs outgrow behaviours such as chewing as they near adulthood, but some do not. Bringing an adult dog into your home requires the same level of vigilance against any potential threat to his heath and safety. An individual dog's behaviours will depend largely on his history; it is your job to protect him as he integrates into your household. An oversight as simple as forgetting to close an outside door could end in disaster.

HOMECOMING DAY

Try to limit activity for your Chihuahua's first day home. You will need to commence housetraining immediately, but all other training should be postponed for at least a day or so. Although it is natural to want to show off your new dog to the neighbourhood, it is wise to postpone walks until he has had all his shots. Puppies are especially susceptible to contagious illnesses. If your dog becomes ill, it can delay his vaccination schedule, as vaccine manufacturers recommend that only healthy dogs be vaccinated.

If you already have another dog in your household, it is best to plan the two's first meeting on neutral territory—a place with which neither dog is familiar. Pay attention to the body language of both dogs, and wait to head home until it seems they are tolerating each other well. Supervision will be necessary for some time, especially if your first dog is a larger breed. Their relationship won't be built in a day, but you want to start off in the best way possible.

SUPPLIES

Here are some supplies you will need when bringing home your tiny treasure.

Feeding Supplies

The first item your Chihuahua will need is a set of dishes—bowls for food and water. There is a vast selection of styles and colours available, but the most important thing to remember is size. When it comes to Chihuahua bowls, bigger is not better. Your Chihuahua needs bowls that are shallow and narrow in diameter, so he can easily reach his food at mealtime and not fall into his water bowl when drinking. You will also likely want bowls that will not tip and are easy to clean, since they need to be washed daily. Stainless steel works best.

Plastic bowls can cause a condition called plastic dish nasal dermatitis. This is a form of contact dermatitis caused by an antioxidant found in plastic or rubber bowls. Dogs fed out of plastic bowls may lose the dark colouring on their nose and lips, often without their owners even knowing the reason. Though not serious, the problem is not just cosmetic—affected dogs may also suffer from inflamed or irritated skin in these areas. If the skin doesn't show any signs of irritation, simply changing the bowls should prevent any future discomfort, but the discolouration may be permanent. If your Chihuahua's nose or lips seem swollen or sore, schedule an appointment with your dog's veterinarian.

One of the most important decisions you will ever make for your Chihuahua is what you will feed him. Your options are many, but any change in your dog's diet must be gradual. Whether you plan to continue with his current regimen or begin a new one, you will need to purchase some of the food the dog is currently eating.

Harness or Collar?

Many breeders recommend using a harness instead of a collar for a Chihuahua due to the dog's particularly small and fragile trachea (windpipe). This, combined with their excitable nature, can cause a Chihuahua to wheeze excessively. This seemingly uncontrollable gagging sound can easily frighten a new Chihuahua owner. Many dogs also seem to prefer the feel of the harness, since its weight is distributed over a larger area of the body. Another advantage of harnesses is that they help prevent escape. Chihuahuas are notorious wrigglers and can be impressive escape artists. This could be of vital concern if you walk your dog in an area with a lot of traffic.

If your dog doesn't seem to mind wearing one, and he doesn't suffer from repeated problems with wheezing, there is no problem with using a collar. Just make sure that the collar you choose is made of a comfortable, lightweight fabric. Also for reasons of safety, always select a fixed-circumference collar, meaning the collar doesn't tighten no matter how hard your dog pulls. A Chihuahua should have no problem tolerating a carefully selected, properly fitting collar for any length of time. There are other reasons, however, that you may want to consider taking the collar off your dog when indoors. Although collars that tighten around the neck pose the greatest threat, any collar left on your Chihuahua all the time is a potential strangling hazard. If your dog will be wearing a collar permanently, make sure to select one with breakaway technology, as it could save your dog's life.

A Perfect Fit

You should be able to easily fit two fingers between your dog's neck and his collar.

The most important thing to remember when selecting either a collar or harness for your Chihuahua is proper fit. Never merely guess your dog's size for these items. If it is too loose, your dog can slip out of it and get away from you. Loose collars and harnesses can also snag on something. If it is too tight, it can make breathing difficult.

When measuring your Chihuahua's neck to determine his collar size, remember that you should be able to fit two fingers comfortably between your dog's neck and the tape. Most harnesses are adjustable and based on your dog's chest measurement. To determine this measurement, place the tape gently around the dog's chest, just behind his front legs—again, placing two fingers between the harness strap and your dog's body. Your dog's collar or harness size will never be the exact measurement, but rather

slightly larger for a comfortable but snug fit.

Harnesses and collars come in an array of materials and designs, many offering matching leads. The most practical fabrics for your Chihuahua are cotton and nylon. Both are washable and relatively durable. Leather, while a wonderful choice for many other breeds, is just too heavy for a Chihuahua.

Lead

Your Chihuahua's lead should also be lightweight and an appropriate length for the area in which the two of you will walk. If you are on the taller side, make sure the lead is long enough for your Chihuahua to walk comfortably alongside you—eight feet is usually sufficient. An overly wide or double-ply lead is a waste for a Chihuahua; it will do little more than weigh too heavily on both your dog and your hands. Nonslip handles are a good idea, as is reflective material for greater visibility if you will be venturing out at night.

Like collars and harnesses, leads are available in a number of styles and materials. Metal link leads are too heavy for Chihuahuas. Choke chains, which can be made of metal or nylon, should never be used with a Chihuahua, due to his small neck.

A versatile option for owners who like to walk in different types of environments is a retractable lead. Offering the dual conveniences of keeping your dog at a short distance when necessary and allowing him to roam a bit in safer settings, a retractable lead saves both space and money. With the touch of a button, you can promptly switch from a 6-foot lead to a 16-foot lead, and back again. It is quite literally several leads in one. These plastic covered reels are available in a number of lengths, colours,

and models—many with comfortable, ergonomic handles. This is also an excellent tool for safely teaching your dog to come when called.

It is very important to remember that you should never yank your Chihuahua's lead, especially when the dog is wearing a collar, as you could unintentionally injure your dog's delicate neck.

Clothes

Your Chihuahua will also need a warm sweater if you live in a cold climate. To find your Chihuahua's sweater size, measure the dog from collar to tail. If you have any trouble finding a small enough garment at your local pet shop, a quick Internet search should yield numerous online retailers, including many that offer hand-knit custom designs. You can even find web sites with instructions on how to knit one yourself. Also available are waterproof raincoats and boots for dogs that especially dislike getting wet while doing their outdoor business.

Crate and Bedding

Whether you choose crate training or another method of housetraining, a crate (complete with a padded liner, usually sold separately) is an incredibly useful and versatile item for most dog owners. For a Chihuahua owner, it is a handy method of transportation that helps keep your dog safe during travel, whether you are taking a quick ride in the car or going on holiday.

Since Chihuahuas are so intensely small, sleeping in his owner's bed can be an extremely dangerous habit; a Chihuahua can suffer a serious injury from a fall from this height. You could also unknowingly roll onto the dog in the night, crushing or suffocating him. With his portable size, your Chihuahua's crate can easily be moved to your bedroom each night, so your dog can be with you, but still in his own safe environment.

Many dogs use crates as their own personal refuge. The den instinct is so strong with most dogs that they consider their crate a haven away from noise, light, and occasionally even people and other animals. Many owners report that their dogs spend time regularly in their crates at various times throughout the day.

When a dog has no such place of his own, he will often seek out a less than ideal spot. A quiet corner of the room may be an acceptable place for your Chihuahua's time alone, but many dogs seek out quarters behind or under furniture where electrical cables or other dangers may be lurking.

If your dog enjoys having a crate, he probably won't need a separate dog bed, but it may be a thoughtful addition if you find your dog moving from room to room with you throughout your day, as so many Chihuahuas do. A soft bed is also a nice idea if you have tile or hardwood floors in your home. Long coat Chihuahuas may enjoy the cool feeling of a bare floor on their bellies, but a short coat will undoubtedly prefer the cosiness of a warm bed.

Since Chihuahuas are so compact themselves, having one or more extra beds won't take up a lot of space in your home.

Fun, Fun, Fun

Just like children, Chihuahuas need toys. Dogs love to play, and Chihuahuas are no exception. From providing a proper outlet for chewing to thrilling your dog with an enticing squeak when they are pounced on, toys can be very important possessions.

Chewing is not an inherently bad behaviour—it actually helps your dog maintain a healthy mouth with a strong jaw and good tooth development. Allowing your Chihuahua to chew appropriate items can help him relieve boredom, frustration, and stress. This is particularly true for dogs that are left alone for an extended period each day. By providing your Chihuahua with suitable chewing toys, you are also teaching your

Your Chihuahua will need a warm sweater if you live in a cold climate.

49

An old slipper can provide hours of enjoyment for a dog, but this can set a bad precedent. Your dog won't necessarily understand the distinction between your old slipper and your brand-new shoes—to a Chihuahua; both will suit his purpose equally well.

dog which items are and are not fair game for his teething pleasure.

Dogs are intelligent beings. Chihuahuas in particular possess excellent problem-solving skills, but mental stimulation is required for them to use and further develop their abilities. Balls that hold and release a special treat when rolled a certain way are one example of toys that can provide the kind of mental stimulation your dog likely desires.

Exercise should also be a big part of play. Although chew toys are intended for quiet times, toys that make noise are designed for throwing, retrieving, and even shaking. Fetch isn't the only game that can be played with balls and squeak toys. Make up your own games as you go along. Avoid simply giving your dog a toy and expecting him to run around with it blissfully by himself. If you find your dog losing interest in toys, it is unlikely that your Chihuahua has outgrown play, but more likely he doesn't want to play alone. Your active involvement helps make play everything it should be—healthy, invigorating fun.

Your biggest challenge may be finding toys that are small enough for your Chihuahua. More than one Chihuahua has been known to proudly drag around an overly large stuffed plaything, but it is vital your dog have at least some toys that he can fit in his tiny mouth. Cat toys sometimes work well, but they must be durable enough for long-term use; otherwise you will find yourself in a constant cycle of replacing them. Smaller versions of popular items such as balls and Frisbees can sometimes be found at pet shops or online, so your Chihuahua can enjoy these universally fun games.

Unless you are feeding your Chihuahua a raw diet, avoid giving your dog real bones. The splinters of real bones can cut your dog's mouth and pierce his intestinal lining with their sharp edges. Bone fragments can also perforate or obstruct the bowel, a potentially fatal situation. The most dangerous bones are cooked ones, particularly chicken bones. When any bone is cooked, it becomes dry and more likely to break apart. This poses a significant choking risk for your Chihuahua.

Grooming Supplies

Most likely your Chihuahua won't need a full grooming session when you first bring him home. It is a good idea, however, to have a few rudimentary tools on hand from the beginning. A soft brush used daily can help familiarise your dog with the grooming routine. It is also a good idea to purchase a bottle of puppy shampoo, since young dogs are prone to accidents during early housetraining. Your dog shouldn't need his first bath right away—unless he gets soiled during such a blunder. In this situation you will be very thankful for having already purchased this item. Wet wipes are another useful cleansing item and may suffice for small accidents.

Make sure you give your Chihuahua appropriate chew toys to help maintain a healthy mouth and relieve boredom.

Identification

Identification, be it an ID tag, tattoo, or microchip, is essential. There are several options from which to choose, and each has their pros and cons.

Tags

Your Chihuahua must have an ID tag that includes your name and telephone number. It is a legal requirement in the UK and it is the quickest means of ensuring that you and your Chihuahua are reunited should you become separated. Tags are readily available at retail pet outlets, mail order catalogues, and online vendors. They come in a variety of shapes, sizes, colours and materials, and easily attach to your dog's collar. You can even find nameplates that attach directly to your dog's collar, eliminating the unmistakable, not to mention frequently annoying, jingling noise produced by multiple tags dangling from a dogs collar.

Microchipping and Tattooing

Many veterinarians suggest having your dog tattooed or microchipped, as well—so he can be conclusively identified for the rest of his life. If your dog is ever lost or stolen and taken to a veterinarian or rescue centre, he will be checked for a tattoo and scanned for a microchip.

A tattoo for a dog looks virtually the same as a human's tattoo and is applied in a similar manner. A unique number in permanent ink is applied with a needle onto the dog's skin—usually on the inside of the right thigh. Since being restrained during this procedure would be both uncomfortable and potentially scary for the animal, most vets recommend that the dog be put under anaesthesia. A good way to avoid an unnecessary anaesthesia is having the tattoo applied when your dog is being spayed or neutered, since he will have to be under anaesthesia for this reason, as well.

There is no need to worry if you plan to show your dog. A tattoo will not disqualify or count against your Chihuahua in the ring. On the contrary, many people involved with this pastime encourage the use of tattooing for safety purposes.

Microchipping involves implanting a tiny electronic device (about the size of a grain of rice) beneath the dog's skin between his shoulder blades. The procedure is as quick and painless as a vaccination and is less expensive than tattooing since anaesthesia is not necessary.

These permanent forms of identification are the safest ways to help ensure that your Chihuahua is returned to you in either situation, but you must register either a tattoo or a microchip with the appropriate directory in order for the related numbers to link your dog to you. For this reason it is also vital that you update your contact information with this agency whenever you move or change phone numbers. Likewise, if you move, inform your new vet that your dog has been microchipped, so the number may be added to his or her records, as well. Once your pet is lost or stolen, it is too late, so if this is something you want done, ask your veterinarian about it during your dog's first visit.

Scheduling Your Dog's First Exam

Don't forget to schedule your dog's first veterinary exam well in advance. Depending on how busy the surgery is, it may be a few weeks before your pup can be seen.

Carrying Bags

Many Chihuahua owners like to carry their dogs everywhere. Although taking them along is rarely a problem, never having your arms free can be. For this reason canine carrying bags have become relatively popular methods of transportation for this totable breed. These bags offer the ease of portability combined with the necessity of safety. Sides are usually constructed with ventilated panels with convertible coverings for privacy or cold weather. Unlike purses, these bags also come with padded bottoms, lead rings, and noncollapsible frames. In addition they offer such owner amenities as fashionable colours and pockets for your wallet and mobile phone, so you have the option of carrying just the one item.

Even though virtually any bag will hold your Chihuahua's weight, not just any bag should do. Allowing your Chihuahua to ride in your pocketbook can be dangerous for several reasons. Since your purse wasn't meant to carry a live animal, it has no openings for breathing if you close it—and if you keep it open, you risk a deadly fall for your dog, hardly worth the cute look of having him peeking out from between the bag's straps. You will also expose your Chihuahua to all the items already in your purse. Your dog could easily be wounded with a pen, or he could decide to make a snack of your lipstick.

TRAVELLING WITH YOUR PORTABLE PET

A microchip or tatoo serves as a permanent form of identification for your dog.

Because Chihuahuas are so small, they can be perfect travel companions, but owners need to do their part to make travelling as

easy as possible for all involved. When making your travel arrangements, locate the names and numbers of several different veterinarians in all areas you will be staying. Keep this information with you at all times throughout your trip. The internet can be a very useful tool for this task; you may even be able to print out maps with detailed directions to the veterinary hospitals of your choosing.

Hotels and Bed and Breakfast

If your travels with your dog include staying at a hotel or a bed and breakfast, call ahead to be sure that they take pets. Many establishments do not accept dogs–even well-behaved Chihuahuas. Some facilities allow dogs in the rooms but may insist that they are kept in a crate. Some larger hotels provide kennel facilities. Many require a refundable pet deposit or a nonrefundable pet fee.

Be a good ambassador for the Chihuahua breed–as well as all dogs–by following hotel and bed and breakfast rules, including never leaving an unattended dog in the room. An otherwise calm dog may become anxious in unfamiliar surroundings. He may chew furniture, shred pillows, urinate, defecate, or annoy other

Canine carrying bags are a great way to transport this totable breed.

visitors with his barking. If you plan to have your Chihuahua sleep on the bed, bring an extra sheet or blanket from home to cover and protect the establishment's bedspread. Without exception, always clean up after your Chihuahua and deposit any messes in designatedbins.

Campsites

Like many hotels, bed and breakfast establishments and self-catering cottages, not all public or private parks and campsites allow dogs. It is highly advisable to call ahead to make sure that dogs are allowed and to find out about any pet surcharges that may be applicable.

Be sure to follow site rules, and do not allow your Chihuahua to intrude on other campers or their animals. It is never wise to leave your Chihuahua unattended or tied up where he can be teased, stolen or attacked by another dog, and there is always the possibility that he may break free and become lost in a strange environment.

Travelling by Car

Holding your Chihuahua safely in your arms during car rides may be pleasing to both of you, but safe is the one thing it isn't. In the event of an accident, your dog's chances of surviving are far greater if he is contained in his crate. Securing a seatbelt around the crate will further protect your dog.

A small soft toy may be comforting to your Chihuahua when travelling. Just remember, one without a squeaker is often best for longer car rides.

Always bring along plenty of drinking water for your Chihuahua, and don't forget a bowl. Collapsible bowls that have been designed specifically for travel are available at most pet shops. These lightweight containers take up little space, so they can be stored in your glove box until needed. If you will be away from home for longer than a few hours, be sure to also bring an adequate supply of your dog's food. Feed your dog lightly before a trip— about one-third its normal amount.

Pooper scoopers aren't exactly made for travel, but small waste bags will serve the same purpose. If your Chihuahua is paper trained and therefore not used to relieving itself outdoors, you may also want to also bring newspapers. Make frequent stops for

Pet Travel Scheme (PETS)

PETS is a system that permits companion animals from certain countries to travel to the UK without undergoing a period of quarantine. This scheme also applies to people in the UK who want to travel with their pets to other European Union countries.

For more information, visit the Department for Environment Food and Rural Affairs' web site at www.defra.gov.uk.

this purpose.

They're not just for babies anymore—baby wipes are handy items for mishaps of all kinds, but can be especially useful when travelling with dogs.

Being prepared is never underrated. Make a list of everything you need for your trip before leaving your house, so your Chihuahua will only be in its crate for as long as necessary. The less time it takes to arrive at your destination, the more you will both enjoy the trip.

Travelling by Air

Most dogs in the UK do not experience air travel. However, with the advent of the Pets Passport Scheme (PETS), which has eliminated the need for six months of quarantine in certain countries. Air travel is now an option for owners who wish to take their dogs overseas on holiday or to compete in international canine events. In America, it is much more common for dogs to travel by air, and there are numerous laws in place for this.

Dogs must travel in airline-approved crates that meet the appropriate regulations for size, strength, sanitation and ventilation. Your Chihuahua may be refused a boarding pass if his kennel does not meet requirements.

When travelling by air, be sure to contact the airline in advance to find out what arrangements can be made for your dog.

Regulations vary from one airline to another, so it is important to always plan ahead. Not all airlines accept dogs, and many limit the number of dogs accepted on each flight. Call the airlines well in advance of your travel plans to schedule flights. Ideally, when booking try to book nonstop flights during the middle of the week, avoiding holiday or weekend travel.

Specific regulations for national and international air travel are available from the Department for the Environment, Food and Rural Affairs..

WHEN YOU CAN'T BE HOME: EMPLOYING CARE FROM OTHERS

Whether you work full time and need regular daycare for your Chihuahua or you take a single holiday a year, you will need someone to look after your dog when you cannot. If you have a responsible friend or family member with whom you feel comfortable leaving your dog when you're away, you might be all set. If that person has other pets or children that could pose a concern, though, you may want to contemplate using a boarding service, or kennel, instead. If it is regular daycare you need, it might be too much to ask of a friend—even the most dependable.

Kennels

Be sure to tour a kennel before deciding it is best for your dog. The most important elements are the cleanliness of the facilities, friendliness of the staff, and the amount of time each day your dog will be taken out of his pen for exercise. A kennel will ask that you show proof of your dog's vaccinations—usually DHLP-P (distemper/parvo combination), and Bordetella (kennel cough). Some also require an intestinal parasite test. These requirements ultimately protect your dog, since all the others dogs have been held to the same standard.

Personal recommendation by a fellow dog lover or your vet is the best starting point in selecting a boarding kennel for your dog. Consider the following points when visiting the establishment:

• How often are the kennels cleaned. How are the kennels cleaned and disinfected between boarders.

• Check the security of the facility. Is it completely fenced? Double fenced? Do the kennel's exercise yards have good latches? Are the fences sturdy and at least six feet high?

• Are the indoor facilities heated? Are the outdoor facilities protected from the weather?

• What will your Chihuahua be sleeping on? Do you need to bring his bed or favourite blanket?

• If you have more than one Chihuahua, will they be housed together?

• How frequently will your Chihuahua be walked or exercised? For how long? What type of exercise? Does someone interact or play with him? Or is he simply left unattended in an exercise yard with or without other dogs?

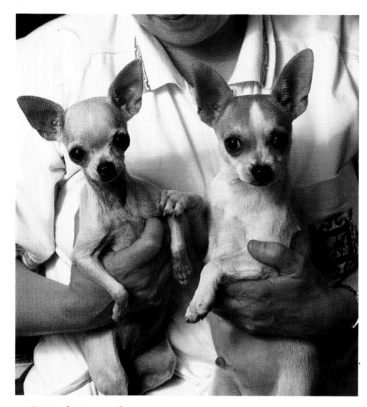

Doggie daycare can be a great option for anyone with a busy schedule.

• What emergency health care provisions are available?
• What are their admission and pick-up hours? What happens if your return is delayed?

Doggie Daycare

Dog daycare differs from boarding in that you utilise a daycare service five days a week, or however many fit your schedule. Daycares also usually spend more time focusing on entertainment and exercise. Most programmes offer both free and organised play times along with walks and other physical activities. The caregiver you choose should use an assessment plan for deciding which dogs are compatible, and therefore allowed supervised interaction. Issues of size, breed, and temperament should all be considered. Not all dogs are suitable candidates for daycare; for the safety of all involved, some are even turned away.

The benefits of placing your dog in daycare are numerous. In addition to exercise and mental stimulation, your dog will receive the added benefit of socialisation. Being around other dogs is excellent experience if you plan to add another dog to your household in the future. If not properly socialised, Chihuahuas, like many breeds, can be very resistant to the idea of other canines in their households. Daycare also offers your dog contact with other humans, which can be extremely helpful if your dog suffers from separation anxiety.

When touring a daycare, you should use the same criteria as when evaluating a boarding service. You will need to show proof of the same vaccinations as for a kennel, but many daycares also require that your Chihuahua be spayed or neutered. Ask a lot of questions. Since your dog will be spending a significant amount of time in this setting, it is vital that you trust the staff.

Although prices can vary by region, the cost of daycare may be higher than that of boarding, since the ratio of staff to dogs is high, but like a children's daycare, the most important matter is that you are leaving your dog in a healthy, safe environment. This is an expanding industry—take time to find a daycare that fits both your budget and comfort level.

Pet Sitters

If your Chihuahua doesn't get along well with other dogs, don't despair. A professional pet sitter or dog walker may be the answer. A pet sitter will come to your home and stay with your dog for a predetermined amount of time while you're away. In many ways this can be even better than daycare, since your dog will receive so much individual attention. A dog walker is similar to a pet sitter in that he or she will come to your home and take your dog for walks while you're away, so he can get out of the house and relieve himself when necessary. If your biggest concern is that you cannot make it home midday to take your dog for his walk, a dog walker may be an ideal solution.

Once again, one of your best resources for referrals is your veterinarian. Interview either a pet sitter or a dog walker thoroughly. Be sure to ask for references and follow up by contacting them. You will trust this person with both your precious Chihuahua and the keys to your home.

Questions to Ask a Kennel or Dog Daycare

- Do staff members possess a broad working knowledge of canine behaviour? What type of training do they receive? Beware of anyone who tells you this isn't a job requiring much experience or instruction.
- What is the staff to dog ratio? The lower the better, but an ideal ratio would be at least one staff member for every 10 dogs.
- Are toy breeds allowed to interact with larger dogs? What is the procedure for introducing new dogs to the programmeme?
- What kinds of discipline are used? Voice reprimands and timeout rooms may be acceptable, but anything physical is not.
- What is the protocol for an emergency? Do the employees know cardiopulmonary resuscitation (CPR) and first aid for pets? If a veterinarian is needed, to whom will your dog be taken?

Chapter 4

FEEDING

the Chihuahua

Never before have there been as many options for feeding your dog as there are today. Today's pet owners spend millions of pounds each year, and they are seeking much more than mere fuel for their pets' systems. They want quality ingredients that promote better canine health, happiness, and appearance. Striving to meet the needs of nearly every size, shape, and age of dog, many pet food companies are rising to this challenge by offering more natural ingredients and far fewer by-products—in some cases none at all.

In addition to the dry and tinned selections of yesterday, there are now additional choices of such specialties as high energy, dental care, and joint-friendly varieties. There are prescription diets for dogs that suffer from allergies or chronic conditions. There are even complete menu planning systems available for those who wish to feed only fresh, raw, or home-cooked food. Deciding which route is best can be overwhelming to a new pet owner. Every company and dog care expert appears to have a different idea of what makes a food healthy. The one thing about which they all seem to agree, though, is that good nutrition is vitally important.

YOUR CHIHUAHUA'S NUTRITIONAL NEEDS

Just like their owners, Chihuahuas have very specific nutritional needs, but these requirements differ significantly between humans and canines. For instance, in order to be healthy, people must eat fruits and vegetables rich in vitamin C, but dogs' bodies produce enough vitamin C on their own, so they do not need to eat foods containing it.

Water

Water is perhaps one of the most underrated dietary sources for good health in both animals and humans. Not only does your Chihuahua need water to survive, he needs water to thrive. Water is the primary vehicle for transporting nutrients throughout your dog's body and removing wastes from his system in the form of urine. It aids in digestion and circulation and is also responsible for regulating your dog's body temperature.

Your Chihuahua needs a balanced diet and plenty of water to keep him healthy.

Protein

Dogs of all ages need protein. Composed of amino acids, protein is the most essential element in the diets of all animals. Puppies and geriatric dogs generally need even greater amounts of protein than adult dogs. This is also the case for extremely active dogs. Foods rich in protein include meat, fish, eggs, dairy products, and legumes. Although vegetables and grains contain protein, these types of protein are more difficult for dogs to digest than those found in meats.

Carbohydrates

Carbohydrates are organic compounds consisting of sugars, starches, and celluloses. Their primary function is to provide energy. Simple carbs are easily digested and absorbed, but complex varieties (starches) need more digestion, and therefore serve as a longer lasting energy source. Common carbohydrates include cereal, pasta, rice, wheat, and vegetables. Like people, dogs need carbohydrates, but feeding the right kind is particularly important. As in human diets, simple sugars are empty calories devoid of nutrients.

Fibre, another carbohydrate, serves many vital functions in your dog's gastrointestinal system—including helping to combat obesity by making a dog feel fuller after his meals. Fibre also helps prevent constipation. Since fibre slows the absorption of sugar, it can even be useful in managing diabetes.

Allergies may be a concern when dealing with carbohydrates, since carbs such as corn, wheat, and soy are common canine food allergens. Too much fibre can also have negative effects. In massive quantities it can prevent the absorption of vitamins and minerals, cause diarrhoea and flatulence (gas), and increase both the volume and density of your dog's stools.

How Much Water Should I Give My Puppy at One Time?

The answer to this one is easy—as much as he wants! You don't have to limit dogs' intake of water the way you sometimes do with food. You also shouldn't worry about only setting out water during scheduled mealtimes. In fact, it's important to your puppy's health that you have fresh, clean water out for him all the time. Dogs of any age need lots of water to help run body processes like circulation, digestion, eliminating waste from the body, and more.

The one case where you might worry about too much water is if your pooch suddenly starts to drink much more than usual, or if he seems constantly thirsty. This could be a sign of a serious health problem, so let your veterinarian know if your pet's drinking habits seem unusual or have changed.

Fats

While too much fat in any diet isn't desirable, dogs need fats, and they need considerably more of them than humans do. The most concentrated source of dietary energy, fats help dogs maintain a healthy temperature, especially during cold weather. They also help keep a dog's skin healthy and make his coat shine. Essential fatty acids are necessary for maintaining normal immune and nervous systems. Finally, fats make food taste better. A food can only benefit your dog if he actually eats it.

Vitamins and Minerals

Vitamins and minerals are necessary in every dog's diet for many purposes. Vitamins help maintain your dog's immune system so it can fight off viral infections and other illnesses. They also aid in the proper absorption of fats and carbohydrates. There are two different kinds of vitamins—fat soluble and water soluble. If a dog is given too much of the former type, the excess will be stored within fatty tissue inside the body, leading to problems even worse than those from deficiencies. Water-soluble vitamins not used by your dog's body are passed in the form of urine.

Trace minerals such as iron and zinc help prevent anaemia, aid in cognitive functioning, and promote healthy coats. It is especially important, though, that vitamins and minerals are provided in very specific amounts and ratios. Minerals such as calcium and phosphorus, for instance, are needed for strong bones and teeth, but when unbalanced they cannot be absorbed and utilised. Too much phosphorus left in your dog's system can also lead to renal (kidney) disease.

Foods Potentially Poisonous to Dogs

- Alcoholic beverages
- Apple seeds
- Apricot stones
- Cherry stones
- Chocolate (baker's, semi-sweet, milk, dark)
- Coffee (grounds, beans, chocolate-covered espresso beans)
- Grapes
- Hops (used in home beer brewing)
- Macadamia nuts
- Mouldy foods
- Mushroom plants
- Mustard seeds
- Onions and onion powder
- Peach stones
- Potato leaves and stems (green parts)
- Raisins
- Rhubarb leaves
- Salt
- Tea (caffeine)
- Tomato leaves and stems (green parts)
- Walnuts
- Yeast dough

DIET OPTIONS
Prepackaged

Prepackaged dog foods come in a variety of mediums—dry (also called kibble), wet, and semi-moist. Dogs eating dry food will generally need more water than those eating wet foods. Dry foods are also more economical and won't spoil if left uneaten in your dog's dish all day. Dogs eating soft foods (usually packaged in tins or rolls) will require more meticulous dental care, as plaque and tartar will build up more rapidly on their teeth. Since semi-moist foods are often more appealing to dogs than dry foods, they may seem like a good compromise, but many of them contain high amounts of sugar. This can be bad for teeth and especially problematic for dogs with diabetes.

Prepackaged foods run the gamut from specialty diets formulated for dogs with increased activity levels, condition diets to help manage such problems as obesity and poor muscle mass, and life-stage diets for puppies, adults, and elderly dogs. Dogs that expel high amounts of energy need more protein, fat, and carbohydrates than their less active counterparts. Overweight dogs will need fewer calories and fat, but keep in mind that eating too much of a weight reduction food can cause your pet to maintain his current weight—or even gain more. Like active dogs, puppies need higher amounts of nutrients in their diets, while geriatric dogs need less fat and more fibre to maintain their systems.

We have known for years that what we put into our bodies is the biggest factor in our own health, but we now know that making equally healthy choices for our canine companions will help them live to share our lives for many years. Of course, a high price does not mean that a food is healthy, but when considering some of the lower-end foods available, it is wise to remember that old adage about getting what you pay for. Cheaper ingredients usually equal lower quality. Even with a breed as small as the Chihuahua, owners may also end up buying more of a cheaper food, since a dog might need to eat more of it to satisfy his caloric needs.

Reading the Label

When comparing brands, go straight to the ingredients lists. Ingredients are required by law to be listed in descending order by weight, so the first ingredient is the most prevalent. You may want to avoid a food that's main ingredients are animal by-products. For example, if the first ingredient is chicken by-products, this means that the largest part of the food includes things like chicken beaks and feet—items not considered fit by the government for human consumption. Even vigilant owners have to use great scrutiny in examining labels, as similar ingredients may be split up and divided into separate subcategories further

Be sure to always provide your Chihuahua with fresh, clean water.

down the list, making it less obvious to the average consumer that the largest percentage may actually be grain and not chicken at all.

Another ingredient that raises concern among pet owners is meal—meat and bone that is ground with most of the water removed. Both meat and poultry by-product meal contain parts of the animals not normally eaten by people. Meal serves as an inexpensive source of protein for dog food companies, but it is a far less efficient form of protein for your Chihuahua. Meal containing large amounts of bone will be difficult for your dog to digest and also be deficient in nutritional value.

Preservatives are another important concern for many owners. Although all prepackaged foods need some kind of preservative, some are believed to be safer than others. Since Chihuahuas ingest more food and preservatives proportionately, they are at a greater risk from the less desirable ones. Among the better preservatives are tocopherols, vitamin-based preservatives used in some canine food brands. It is important to note that foods containing these natural preservatives have a shorter shelf life than those containing other kinds, especially after a bag has been opened.

Synthetic preservatives such as butylated hydroxyanisole (BHA), butylated hydroxytoluene (BHT), and ethoxyquin have all come under particular scrutiny in recent years. Studies have shown that

Read the ingredients on the pet food label before deciding to feed it to your Chihuahua.

very high levels of BHA can cause tumours in the forestomachs of rats, mice, and hamsters. Since there has been no data collected relating to animals lacking a forestomach, and dog foods contain such a minute percentage (0.02 percent of the fat content only), both of these preservatives are currently allowed in dog foods.

When reading a pet food label, look for the manufacturer's phone number. Although companies are only legally required to print their names and addresses on the packages, customers should be able to call with any questions they may have. Many dog food companies also list extensive nutritional information (including customer service e-mail addresses) on their web sites.

Keep It Fresh

It is highly important to keep your dog's food fresh. Tinned food should be refrigerated immediately once opened. If you store dry food in anything other than its original bag, be sure to wash the container whenever you add new food. Fat can settle to the bottom and spoil, contaminating the fresh food and possibly making your pet sick.

Plastic food storage bins are an ideal choice for owners who like to stock up on dry dog food. These inexpensive containers are available in a variety of shapes and sizes and can often be stacked for added convenience.

Since it will take your Chihuahua so long to consume food purchased in bulk, you may want to use a larger container in a more remote spot (such as a basement or garage), and keep a more modest amount of food in a handier location, such as your kitchen cupboard or worktop. If this is the case, you have many choices. Ceramic, glass, and plastic containers are all available in a wide array of designs to match your kitchen's décor. If you choose a ceramic container, though, be certain it is lead free. A good way to be sure is to only purchase items intended for human use. These should be classified as high fire and table quality.

Some plastic storage systems are designed to mount on your wall, making it easy for you to dispense a predetermined amount of food at each meal. These hanging bins usually hold a moderate amount a food and are a good compromise for those with limited space for buying in bulk.

Whatever type of container you choose, make sure it is tightly sealed when stored, or your Chihuahua (and a number of less desirable creatures) may find their way into it. Air can also permeate loosely fitting lids, drastically shortening the shelf life of your dog's food. To help ensure freshness, always check the best before date printed on the package, and never buy more food than your Chihuahua will consume by this date.

Raw Food

Often referred to by its acronym, the BARF diet (short for bones and raw food) may seem like a throwback to the old days of tossing your dog bones from the butcher, but raw vegetables, raw eggs, and dairy foods are also included in this plan, in addition to the raw meats and bones. Unlike prepared foods, raw diets retain a food's natural enzymes and antioxidants that are destroyed by the heat processing of prepared foods.

Proponents of this regimen claim that their dogs' coats are shinier, their teeth are cleaner, and their overall health is better than before eating these foods exclusively. Although this diet does most closely resemble the natural diet of wild dogs, many veterinarians are more concerned about choking and internal injuries that may result from the bones, especially chicken bones since they can be extremely small and are notorious for their splintering qualities.

The BARF diet is often more economical than buying premium prepackaged foods, but to ensure freshness, owners must shop more often for smaller quantities of food. Careful research and planning are also necessary for adequate variety of sufficient nutrients—one of the biggest assets of this kind of diet. Even with all the plausible advantages, though, the BARF diet is not ideal for most Chihuahuas. This breed's smaller digestive system puts them at an increased risk for bones being lodged in their intestines. Bones

Don't Feed Your Chihuahua Cat Food!

Although it may be tempting to feed your Chihuahua the same food as your cat, don't. Cat food lacks many of the nutrients a dog needs, and your dog will likely have a hard time digesting it. Genuine carnivores, cats proportionately require far more meat (and calories) in their diets than dogs. Classified as omnivores, dogs need a larger variety of foods in their diets. Although protein is a must, dogs in fact do not need to eat meat.

Vegetarian Dogs?

Some dog owners and veterinarians insist that dogs need meat. While it is true that meats provide some of the most readily available and easily digestible protein, there are other options. If you prefer to feed your Chihuahua a vegetarian diet, there are many choices available. A vegetarian diet can include any of the items from a home-cooked regimen, with the obvious exception of animal products.

can also cause broken teeth, which can negatively affect your dog's eating habits indefinitely.

Home-Cooked

Some Chihuahua owners think the best way to make sure that their dogs receive all their nutrients is by cooking their pets' meals themselves. Home-cooked canine diets can be especially healthy, providing that owners follow through with their good intentions. In order for home-cooked diets to be nutritious, they must include many different kinds of foods—including meats, grains, and vegetables—and the right amount of each one.

Like the BARF diet, one of the biggest advantages of home cooking is variety. While we may not initially believe that our dogs need variety, imagine your own diet if humans ate the same meal each and every day for their entire lives. We prefer to eat many different foods, and dogs likely do, too. Even if you feed your Chihuahua a prepackaged food, you can still utilise home-cooked foods as healthy additions to his diet.

Many home-cooked diets include rice, which can also be very helpful in managing canine digestive problems. Other healthy canine foods include broccoli, carrots, and leafy green vegetables. Raw cut-up fruits may be offered occasionally. Meat, fish, and eggs are all excellent sources of protein, but eggs (either raw or cooked) should be given less frequently—no more than two or so per week. The benefits and liabilities of including dairy products in a canine diet is still a topic of much discussion, since many dairy foods aren't highly digestible for dogs, but cottage cheese and yogurt both can add valuable calcium to a home-cooked regimen without posing many digestive issues.

Never assume you have all your dog's nutritional bases covered without first getting the input of your veterinarian. He or she can point you towards the best resources for canine home cooking. Remember, also, that just as you can supplement a dog's prepackaged diet with a small amount of home-cooked food, you can supplement a home-cooked meal plan with a quality commercial food. By feeding both kibble and healthy home-cooked foods you can offer your Chihuahua the best of both worlds.

Specialty Diets

If your Chihuahua experiences a serious medical condition, your veterinarian may suggest placing your dog (either temporarily or permanently) on a special diet. Available only through vets, these prescription diets can be very effective in dealing with a variety of problems including allergies, gastrointestinal conditions, and even kidney disease.

Canine food allergies are among the most common reasons some dogs require special diets. Signs of a food allergy can include itching, digestive disorders, or even respiratory distress. Diagnosing an allergy can be difficult, since your veterinarian will need to rule out other more obvious causes of the symptoms first. It may take several months to isolate the particular origin of a dog's allergic reaction.

Dogs can be allergic to any food or ingredient, but common canine food allergens include:

- protein (particularly from certain meat sources)
- milk
- eggs
- whey
- corn
- soy

FREE FEEDING OR SCHEDULED FEEDING?

Opinions differ as to whether a dog should be fed on a set schedule or if free feeding (leaving food available at all times) is a better choice. There are advantages to each method, but much depends on the habits of the individual dog. While free feeding can lead to obesity in dogs inclined to overeat, eating several smaller meals throughout the day is a healthier option than two larger ones usually provided by scheduled feeding. It is also considerably more convenient to free feed, since you just have to make sure to clean your dog's dishes daily, replenishing them with fresh food and water at this time. If you choose the route of free feeding, never simply top off your dog's food and water bowls at feeding time. To prevent your dog from ingesting harmful germs and bacteria that can build up on his dinnerware, wash your dog's dishes every day. You may find it convenient to purchase two sets of bowls for your Chihuahua, so he always has a clean set ready when his other set is being washed.

Scheduled feeding has its advantages as well. It is particularly

If you have the time, home cooking is another option for feeding your Chihuahua.

difficult to housetrain a puppy when you aren't able to keep track of what is going into his system and when, so schedules can be helpful, at least in the beginning. If you plan to board your Chihuahua, or have friends care for him when you are away, it may be wise to keep your dog on a schedule. This will help make feeding easier for all involved. If you prefer that your dog eat several smaller meals throughout the day, this can certainly be accomplished without resorting to free feeding. Just be sure to divide the total amount of food among the number of meals instead of increasing your dog's overall food intake. If your dog is eating too much, this will negate the benefits of the schedule.

To change your Chihuahua from a free-feeding regimen to a more structured schedule, begin by offering at least four meals a day. Once your dog becomes accustomed to the new schedule, you may choose to decrease the number of meals down to two or three. The most important thing is that you only feed your Chihuahua at the selected meal times, while making sure your Chihuahua doesn't go too long without food. If an abrupt change is made to only a couple of meals each day, a dog that is accustomed to free feeding may not eat when food is offered, but suffer a seizure from hypoglycaemia before his next meal. Also, beware of offering your dog snacks between meals during the transition, as these can sabotage your efforts.

AGE-APPROPRIATE FEEDING
Puppies

Puppies not only need consistent feeding schedules, but they also need higher amounts of nutrients in their diets. Puppies from toy breeds like the Chihuahua have different nutritional needs from

Sample Feeding Schedule for the Different Phases of Your Chihuahua's Life

PUPPIES LESS THAN FOUR MONTHS

Chihuahua puppies need three meals per day—in the morning, at midday, and in the early evening. Water should be offered with each meal and then once more a short time after the last meal of the day. While housetraining, be sure to remove your puppy's water bowl one to two hours before bedtime.

PUPPIES BETWEEN FOUR MONTHS AND ONE YEAR

Around the time older puppies are transitioned to adult food, they should also be switched to just two meals per day—eliminating the midday meal. Once housetraining is mastered, water can be offered at all times. Watch your dog for excessive drinking, though, as this might be a sign of a medical problem.

ADULT DOGS

Adult dogs should also be fed two meals per day, but variety can be added by offering a mix of wet and dry food or some raw vegetables to either meal. Since dogs' metabolisms slow as they get older, stick to only healthy treats and swap to a weight reduction diet if your dog becomes overweight.

SENIOR DOGS

Dogs sometimes lose their zest for eating as they age. Try offering several smaller meals each day or warming up your dog's wet food to make eating more fun. Since raw vegetables may be more difficult for your older dog to chew, try offering softer treats like cottage cheese or an occasional hard-boiled egg instead.

those of larger dogs. They need even more protein, fat, calcium, and phosphorus per pound than their more massive counterparts, so be sure to feed a puppy diet specifically formulated for smaller breeds.

Chihuahuas and other toy breeds have a higher metabolic rate per pound and reach maturity considerably faster than larger dogs. A dog who is done growing doesn't need the same amount of calories, fat, and protein as a younger puppy. For this reason, their puppy diets should be discontinued earlier than the typical one-year period recommended for other breeds. Talk to your vet about the best time to switch to an adult diet for your dog. Many owners make the transition around the same time their dogs are spayed or neutered.

Adults

Your Chihuahua's adult diet should differ from his puppy formula chiefly in its amount of protein. The size of the kibble in most puppy foods is smaller than that of regular adult foods, but for your Chihuahua you will also want an adult food that is relatively tiny, so your dog doesn't have any trouble eating it.

When making the transition from puppy food to adult, start off

Dine With Each Other

In the hustle and bustle of our demanding lives, we often overlook the significance of our daily meals. Not only do we regularly feed both our pets and ourselves food we willingly label as junk, we tend to swallow much of it while standing, reading the latest news headlines, or watching the clock (or worse, the television). We have forgotten how enjoyable it is to prepare healthy food for the people (and animals) we love—and then sit and eat together.

Talking to your Chihuahua pleasantly as you prepare his nightly meal can make dinner an inviting time for you both. Instead of feeding the dog before or after the human family members, try timing your meals so you may all eat together. You just might find that your once picky eater decides to lick his dish clean, contentedly digesting his food as the entire family discusses the day's events.

If you eat in the dining room, move your dog's dishes to that room as well. You don't necessarily even need to speak at all. There is a meditative quality to sharing a meal with those you love. The most important part is that you are spending this special time together—nourishing both body and soul.

slowly. Gradually replace your Chihuahua's puppy food with adult food. The first week replace just 25 percent, the next change to 50 percent, and so on until the transition is complete. This is a good method to use whenever you change your dog from one kind of food to another, as the canine digestive system can react poorly to abrupt changes.

Seniors

Unless your dog gains too much weight or is beset with a chronic condition, he should be able to remain on his adult feeding regimen until he reaches senior status—between 7 and 10 years of age. Since Chihuahuas age more gracefully than many other breeds, you might not notice signs of ageing in your dog until he is even older than this. Once you notice the signs, however, it is time to consider a diet designed to ease the pains of ageing.

Many changes accompany ageing. A slower metabolism and decreased activity level both make it easier for your older dog to gain weight, so a diet with fewer calories at this time will help protect your dog from heart disease, diabetes, and even orthopaedic injuries that can often result from added weight. A high-fibre content can help move ageing bowels more regularly. If your older dog has trouble chewing hard foods, you may wish to change to a softer food at this time. Conversely, if your Chihuahua's teeth are in good shape, you might want to feed a senior diet that is also dental friendly, since healthy teeth and gums will be especially important as your dog continues to age.

SUPPLEMENTATION

Your dog should always eat foods rich in vitamins and minerals, but some nutrients may be added to his diet in the form of supplements as either preventive measures or natural ways of managing certain health conditions. Glucosamine, for example, has been shown to be extremely helpful in managing arthritis. While many quality dog foods contain glucosamine, the amounts are usually minimal. Some supplements can also degrade as a result of the heat and pressure of manufacturing.

Other common canine supplements include vitamin E, C, D, and B-complex. Vitamin E can improve coat quality. Together vitamins C and D help make collagen, which strengthens tendons and ligaments. B-complex vitamins help maintain nerve function. Often touted for their healing properties, wheat grass and spirulina have also become extremely popular in the canine supplement community.

Just because a substance is a naturally occurring element, however, does not necessarily mean it is safe. Never give any dog any supplement without the prior approval of the animal's veterinarian. Due to their exceptionally small size, Chihuahuas especially can become seriously ill if given an inappropriate supplement—whether natural or not. Selenium, for example, is a trace element that can be beneficial to the canine heart, but it can be toxic to dogs in great amounts. A dosage of 200 mg may be reasonable for a large dog, but this would be way too much for your Chihuahua.

Puppies need consistent feeding schedules and higher amounts of nutrition than adult Chihuahuas.

OBESITY

Whoever said that an ounce of prevention is worth a pound of cure might well have had a dog's weight in mind. Like people, dogs gain weight far more easily than they lose it, but it is never too late to change. The most common causes for canine obesity are overeating and lack of exercise. Chihuahuas often surprise their owners with their fervent love of food—and their related tendency to become overweight. Obesity can be a life-threatening problem

Common Diseases and Injuries Related to Obesity

- Arthritis
- Cruciate ligament injury
- Diabetes
- Gastrointestinal problems
- Heart disease
- Kidney disease
- Luxating patella
- Musculoskeletal diseases
- Respiratory problems
- Tracheal collapse

for any breed, but is of special concern to a dog this tiny, as the addition of just a pound (.45 kg) can increase a Chihuahua's size substantially. Occasionally, an underlying medical condition such as a thyroid problem may be at the root of the issue, so talk to your vet before starting a new diet and exercise programme for your dog.

Once a medical cause has been ruled out, the first thing you need to do is change your Chihuahua's food. Although you can simply reduce the amount of your dog's current food, by changing to a diet food you will simultaneously be lowering the amounts of protein, vitamins, and minerals your dog is receiving along with the fat and calories. Unless your dog is on a prescription diet, it is better to change to a weight reduction dog food formula. If you feed a raw or home-cooked diet, you will want to lower the fat and increase the fibre your dog is eating; talk to your vet about which foods can best help you accomplish this. Effectively changing your dog's diet also includes eliminating any high-calorie snacks you may have been feeding in the past, and all members of the household must abide by the new rules.

Exercise will also be a necessary part of lowering your Chihuahua's weight, but changes in this area must be gradual. If your dog is not used to going for walks at all, suddenly taking him for several brisk walks in one day could lead to overexertion, joint pain, and even a heart attack. Walking your dog for a reasonable amount of time each day is also far better for his health than having one overly intense exercise session only once a week. You may want to begin by increasing your dog's indoor play time as a way of warming up for adding outdoor walks later. Exercise tolerance will increase as your dog begins to lose his extra weight. You might even find that your former couch potato enjoys more structured forms of exercise, such as agility.

The very worst thing an owner can do is to ignore the problem of obesity. There is a joke among humans that the best day of the week to start a diet is tomorrow. Your Chihuahua may be resistant to the change at first, but if you start working on reducing his weight today, you and your beloved dog will have far more tomorrows to enjoy together.

The healthy weights of different dogs will vary depending on such factors as gender, genetics, and activity level. Although no Chihuahua should weigh much more than 6 pounds (2.7 kg), even

5 pounds (2.3 kg) could be considered overweight for a dog of extremely tiny stature. What is most important is that your adult Chihuahua maintains the weight that is most healthy for him. In addition to a higher number on the scale, signs that your dog has gained too much weight may include waddling when walking, shortness of breath after minimal exercise, and your not being able to easily feel his ribs.

Treats

One of the quickest ways to add unnecessary weight to your Chihuahua is offering the wrong kinds of treats. Although it may be fun to share crisps or ice cream with your dog, these foods are even more detrimental to your Chihuahua than they are to you because of his diminutive size. Many human foods can make acceptable canine treats, but junk foods (high-calorie snacks lacking nutritional value) are not among them. Try to limit these foods in your dog's diet—or better still, don't offer them at all.

Healthy human foods that may be shared include unbuttered popcorn, pretzels, unflavoured rice cakes, apple or orange slices, and seedless watermelon chunks. Raw vegetables such as carrots, celery, and green peppers can serve the dual purposes of tasty snacks and a means of helping to keep your Chihuahua's teeth clean. Even healthy treats, when given in large quantities, though, can cause weight gain. Remember, treats don't always have to be edible. One of the best rewards you can offer your Chihuahua is time spent together—maybe even burning off some of those tasty treats.

THE WELL-MANNERED CHIHUAHUA
Begging

Dogs do not learn how to beg on their own; this behaviour is taught and ingrained by their owners whenever human food is offered from the table. Some owners of begging dogs argue that they hardly ever give out treats from the table, but this may explain more than they think. A rudimentary look at psychology reveals that intermittent rewards actually reinforce behaviours better than consistent rewards.

This unpleasant behaviour problem can be corrected, but it requires an owner's complete dedication to retraining the animal. This doesn't mean that you may never share table scraps with your Chihuahua if you want to prevent begging. You must simply approach the task in a different way. First, never give in to begging. You must ignore your dog whenever he implores you to share your meal. Second, whenever you do share a special food with your dog, always place it directly into your dog's dish, preferably from the worktop and not the table.

If your Chihuahua is a tenacious beggar, consider giving him something else to do when the rest of the family is eating. At dinnertime, feed your dog at the same time as everyone else. If the begging usually begins just after your dog finishes his own meal, try offering him a special chew toy at this time. Also offer it at other times you are eating and want to redirect your dog's attention. A flavoured dental bone can help keep your Chihuahua's teeth sparkling clean while also offering you some peace and quiet.

Don't feed your Chihuahua junk food—habits like that may lead to obesity.

Certainly begging is not the only less–than–desirable behaviour your Chihuahua might adopt. Drooling is another rather unpleasant canine behaviour, but unlike begging, this behaviour is very normal—and even healthy. If your Chihuahua's tendency to drool at the sight and smell of your food is making dinnertime less enjoyable for you, however, it may be time to consider moving your dog to another room when you eat. In extreme situations drooling can be a sign of illness—so mention it to your vet if you notice any increase in frequency, or if your dog who has never before been a drooler suddenly seems to have become one.

Food Aggression

One canine behaviour that no owner wants to be confronted with is food aggression. Many factors can contribute to an individual dog's tendency towards aggressive behaviour. Genetics certainly play a part, particularly in dogs whose lines include excessive inbreeding. Hormone levels can also affect a dog's temperament, especially for intact males and unspayed females in the midst of a heat cycle. An even bigger factor, however, is socialisation. A dog who is properly socialised in the earliest stages of his life is far less likely to act aggressively over food or anything else.

Puppies should be hand-fed by all household members, including children. Teach your dog to take food gently without snapping or grabbing it from you. Sit with your dog while he eats on his own, gently placing your hand in his bowl from time to time. If your Chihuahua reacts negatively, this can be a defining moment.

Feeding your dog by hand at an early age will help to prevent food aggression as he grows older.

Children and Dogs

It is important not to underestimate the damage a toy breed can inflict. As small as they may be, Chihuahuas may bite and wound even a much-loved family member. Children are especially vulnerable to dog bites, so be sure to teach your child that it is never okay to tease a dog. Any dog can bite when provoked.

Teach your child some basic obedience commands, and practice them together, instructing your dog to sit before putting his bowl down, for example. Viewed through a dog's pack mentality, children are often considered the easiest family members to challenge for a more dominant position in the household hierarchy. If taught proper consideration and also empowered with the tools to assert themselves appropriately, your children can enjoy positive relationships with your Chihuahua while still maintaining their proper positions as your dog's superiors.

If tolerated, this growling and other threatening behaviours will lay a foundation for further aggression in other areas of your dog's life. A dog will not outgrow aggression on his own; he must be taught.

Food aggression is an act of dominance. Some owners love their Chihuahuas so much that they tend to spoil them, but constant praise for virtually nothing more than being cute can lead your dog to a superiority complex. When your dog growls at you for getting too close to his bowl, he is actually attempting to train you to stay away from his food. Your dog needs to be shown that you are the alpha dog in the household. In the wild the alpha dog always eats first, so it may be productive to start feeding your dog after your own meal until you are able to correct this unacceptable behaviour.

If your dog attempts to guard his food from you, remove the bowl at once, and begin feeding exclusively by hand. If the dog only acts aggressively towards one family member, make that person the one in charge of feeding. A dog literally won't bite the hand that feeds him. When the dog takes a piece of food gently, praise the good behaviour.

When you are ready to return to feeding from a bowl, make a point of moving your dog's food dish around the room every so often. This will help eliminate protectiveness over a specific eating spot. Most importantly, never use physical punishment as a means of correcting your dog's aggression. Striking any animal can cause serious injury, but toy breeds can be especially hurt by this kind of punishment. Hitting will likely also stimulate further aggression instead of discouraging it. If your dog has already become extremely aggressive around food, you may need to consult your veterinarian or an animal behaviourist for help in correcting the problem.

Preventing food aggression is far easier than correcting the problem later. To show your Chihuahua that having people around his food can be a positive experience, occasionally add a special treat to his bowl in the middle of his meal. Work towards discouraging aggression even when food is not involved. Allowing your dog to bite you during play can set an inappropriate example and lead your dog to think that biting might be tolerated in other situations. Teaching general obedience is an excellent way to show your Chihuahua his proper place in the family before aggression can become a problem.

FOOD AS A TRAINING TOOL

One of the most effective means of dog training is using edible rewards. Some owners refuse to resort to what they consider bribery to train their dogs, but few can deny the usefulness of food as a motivator nonetheless. While you may be able to teach your Chihuahua commands by using verbal praise alone, getting your dog to repeat the tasks will likely require more than words alone. The value of praise should certainly not be overlooked, but owners should also understand that praise comes in many forms.

If you are concerned about potential weight gain, there are a few things you can do to prevent training treats from causing excess weight. First and foremost, only use healthy snacks. Treats should be divided into small, bite-sized portions. Sensible choices include cubed chicken or cheese. Dog biscuits and raw vegetables such as carrots may serve the reward purpose, but the amount of time your dog needs to chew these items can easily distract him from the tasks at hand. Chapter 6 has more information training your Chihuahua with food as a positive reinforcement.

Using treats as a reward can be a great way to positively train your Chihuahua.

Chapter

5

GROOMING
Your Chihuahua

Although nature gave Chihuahuas their exceptional good looks, it is good nurturing that will help keep them healthy. Grooming is a basic responsibility of dog ownership for any breed. As many Chihuahua enthusiasts have discovered, however, it can also be a very special bonding time for both dog and owner.

The Chihuahua is considered a natural dog. Compared to many others, he is also a relatively low-maintenance breed, as his coat does not require trimming of any sort. Whether you own a long or smooth coat Chihuahua, though, a moderate amount of regular grooming will be necessary.

When many people think of dog grooming, the first two things that spring to mind are brushing and bathing—and for good reason. These are two fundamental elements to keeping your dog attractive and clean. They are not the only ones, though. Keeping your Chihuahua's nails, teeth, eyes, and ears in proper shape is just as, if not more, important.

GROOMING AS A HEALTH CHECK

In addition to keeping your dog clean, grooming is an ideal opportunity to examine your dog for any health problems. Always begin brushing your dog with your bare hands, carefully observing any changes in his hair and skin. The best defence against most canine diseases and illnesses is early detection.

Always be on the lookout for cuts and sores, rashes and bumps, and fleas and ticks. Have any abnormal growths checked by your veterinarian. Most will be benign (harmless), but even malignant (cancerous) tumours can often be successfully removed when caught early.

Flea and Tick Removal

Remove fleas with a fine-tooth comb and drop them into soapy water. Embedded ticks can be tricky, but it is vital to remove the entire body, as well as the head. Using a pair of sterilised tweezers, grasp the tick's body and start pulling it away from your Chihuahua's skin. Do keep steady pressure on it, but the object at this point is simply getting the tick to let go, so be careful that you don't squeeze too tightly. Jiggle the tick, but don't rotate it, as

Grooming Supplies for Your Chihuahua

- Soft bristle brush
- Damp cloth
- Rubber comb
  (for long coats)

you don't want to separate the head from the body.

If the tick will not release after several minutes, apply a drop of alcohol on it. You may need to repeat this process, but it is usually a successful means of getting even the most stubborn tick to let go. Once the tick is completely out, drop it in a container of alcohol. If you cannot remove the tick—or if you can only get part of it out, seek help from your veterinarian.

Skin Care

Since dogs have fur, owners might not often consider the importance of proper canine skin care. Basic canine skin care involves maintaining the dog's coat while keeping an eye on both hair and skin. Irritated skin leads to scratching, which can then lead to infection. Bathing too frequently or using harsh shampoos can lead to itchy, dry skin, and allergies can cause skin rashes.

The most common canine skin allergen is fleas, but your Chihuahua can also suffer from inhaled allergens (such as pollen), as well as food allergies. Whereas a human's reaction to pollen may be watery eyes, a runny nose, and sneezing, a dog's reaction is itchy skin. Older dogs are more likely to develop both eye infections and skin allergies, since allergens that weren't previously a problem can bother dogs more as they age. An intradermal skin test (a procedure performed by a veterinarian during which small amounts of allergens are injected beneath the dog's skin) can help isolate the specific cause of your dog's allergy. Blood tests, while less expensive, have proved to be less reliable.

GOOD HABITS START EARLY

The best way to help your dog enjoy the grooming process is by introducing all the different elements as early as possible. Hopefully, this process was started before you even brought your new Chihuahua home. A puppy who is raised with regular baths, brushing, and nail clippings will quickly learn that these are normal parts of his routine, and he will resist the procedure much less as an adult dog.

To help your Chihuahua find the grooming process as stress-free as possible, be gentle but consistent in your approach. Start with a brief brushing session when you are both relaxed, extending the duration gradually each day until your dog seems at ease with completing the task. Always try to end on a positive note, and reward your Chihuahua for cooperating. Keep in mind that your dog's comfort level should take precedence over results; it may take several days to complete a full grooming session while your Chihuahua is a puppy. If you make it fun, clipping just one nail a day or getting your puppy to tolerate brushing for a couple of minutes can be a rewarding experience for both of you.

BRUSHING

Brushing your Chihuahua not only helps make his coat look radiant—it also helps keep your dog clean and in need of fewer baths. If your Chihuahua could talk, he would tell you that brushing feels pretty darn good, too.

Brushing will loosen dirt and dead hair that get trapped beneath the fur. It will also help prevent shedding, as well as matting. In addition to dirt, the dust and debris in your Chihuahua's fur can contain any number of toxic contaminants—everything from furniture polish and floor cleaners to chemicals used on lawns and gardens. For this reason, it is much better to brush this debris out of your dog's coat than for your Chihuahua to attempt licking it out and risk swallowing it during self-grooming.

Brushing will loosen dirt and dead hair that get trapped beneath the fur.

Shedding

While the Chihuahua doesn't shed excessively, periodic shedding is a normal part of the breed's hair growth cycle. Approximately every 125 to 135 days, the dog's hair will grow, rest, die, and ultimately fall out. This is when the dog will blow, or shed, his coat. This most intense shedding time usually occurs in the spring. Dogs typically grow heavier winter coats for

If your Chihuahua resists being brushed, make sure you are being gentle and using a soft brush.

protection against the cold, but this seasonal growth is sometimes inhibited by artificial light. By simply living indoors, your Chihuahua may shed at any time.

How to Brush Your Chihuahua

The most important thing to remember about brushing is that it should always be done before bathing, since mats and tangles worsen when wet. A soft bristle brush is the best type to use for your tiny friend. Be gentle with the brushing, but make sure that the bristles are reaching the skin. Some owners of shorthaired breeds assume that their dogs don't need regular brushing, but this isn't the case. Wiping your smooth coat Chihuahua with a damp cloth is sufficient for his daily routine, but brushing should be done at least three times a week to help ensure good skin and coat health. Long coats should be brushed daily. Remember, frequent brushing means less hair on your carpet, furniture, and clothing.

With the soft bristle brush, start by brushing your Chihuahua's fur in the opposite direction of hair growth to help loosen dead hair; then continue brushing in the natural direction of the hair streams. Facing your Chihuahua away from you, begin with the dog's back, brushing from his tail to his neck, and then moving on to his sides, underside of neck, legs, chest, belly, and finally the tail. Be sure to pay special attention to such tangle-prone areas as behind the ears, under the elbows, and in the britches (the hair on the upper rear area of your dog's legs). A rubber comb is useful for keeping long coats tangle free. With their extra hair in the form of leg furnishings, plumed tails, and fringed ears, long coats are especially vulnerable to snarls.

If your Chihuahua resists being brushed, make sure you are being gentle and using a soft brush. Though useful for removing mats, wire brushes can hurt a dog's skin if too much pressure is

applied. Brush first with your fingers alone to show your Chihuahua how good brushing can feel.

If your Chihuahua's hair starts matting, this is a sign that it isn't being brushed often enough. Always try brushing the mat out of the hair before resorting to cutting, as the shorter hairs left after cutting are often more prone to matting. If you must cut, be sure to follow up by combing the area daily. Some pet shops offer a tool called a mat splitter to help with minor mats; this tool helps shred the mat for easy removal. You can also place a comb between the mat and skin, cutting only the hair above the combs' teeth, so as not to cut the dog. If the mat is a serious one, though, it is best to bring your Chihuahua to a professional groomer to help prevent pain or injury to the dog during removal.

BATHING

With adequate brushing your Chihuahua should only need a bath about once a month. Since shampoos can strip the coat of natural oils that moisturise the coat and skin, your goal should be bathing your Chihuahua only when necessary. Be sure to use a moisturising shampoo, and always be on the lookout for dry, flaky skin—a sign of overly frequent bathing.

Shampoos and Conditioners

When selecting a dog shampoo, resist the temptation to use a human product. Owners may think they are giving their Chihuahuas the very best by sharing their own designer products, but even the best human shampoos are not best for dogs. Compared to the acidic nature of human skin, a dog's skin has a slightly alkaline pH, so the chemicals in our shampoos can actually harm our dogs. Their skin is also thinner than ours, leaving it even more vulnerable to irritation.

If your dog shows any signs of a skin reaction (redness, rash, or constant itching) after using any product, consult your veterinarian—your dog may need a medicated shampoo. Just as the selection of human products keeps growing, so does the assortment of canine shampoos, including tear-free, anti-tangle, whitening, oatmeal, and anti-dandruff varieties. Canine conditioners are also available and can help your Chihuahua's hair and skin stay soft and smooth for weeks after bathing. You can also purchase timesaving combination shampoo-conditioners, as well as leave-in conditioners.

Are Grooming Tables a Good Idea?

Although a grooming table might be helpful as a sturdy, nonslip surface for grooming, consider the cost and size in relation to your Chihuahua before investing in one. Unless you plan to show your dog, you may not use it enough to justify the purchase. You can easily brush your Chihuahua in your lap, on the floor, or just about anywhere you both feel comfortable. Beware of high places, such as conventional tables or counters, though. Unlike a grooming table, these places will not have a safety harness, and a fall from this height could be catastrophic.

Between baths you may use a waterless shampoo for maintenance; these rinse-free products are sold in most pet shops and provide dog owners with a fast and easy way to clean their pets. Though not a substitute for a complete bath, these products are useful for spot cleaning, bathing after a surgical procedure, or for use on cold winter days.

Where to Bathe Your Chihuahua

As with a grooming table, a separate bathing tub might be helpful to some, but not others. Many Chihuahua owners use their bath to bathe their Chihuahua, while others find that the kitchen sink more than accommodates this pint-sized breed. Use extreme caution when using the sink, though, as there are risks associated with jumping or falling. Regardless of the basin type you choose, it is a good idea to place your Chihuahua on a nonskid mat to prevent any injuries from slipping.

How to Bathe Your Chihuahua

When the time comes for bathing your Chihuahua, the first thing you should to do is gather all the necessary supplies—shampoo and conditioner, a cup or spray nozzle for rinsing, a washcloth, cotton balls, mineral oil, and towels. Once your dog is in the midst of his bath, you won't be able to leave his side to retrieve something you've forgotten, so make sure you don't miss anything. Next, make sure the room is warm; Chihuahuas get cold very easily. Finally, when you think you're all ready to start the water running, take your dog for a bathroom break. This is especially important if your dog relieves himself outdoors, since the dog should be kept inside until thoroughly dry. If you live in a wintry climate, you may want to plan the bath for early in the day, so your Chihuahua is sure to be completely dry by evening when it is even colder.

Like the room, the water should be warm, but not hot. The old fashioned method of testing a human baby's bath water with your elbow is an excellent way of making certain the temperature is right for your Chihuahua. Warm water opens hair follicles, which will help loosen dead hair.

Before wetting your Chihuahua, place a cotton ball gently inside each ear, to help prevent getting water inside them. Next, wet the dog's entire body, including his undercoat, but not the head and face. Using just a few drops of shampoo, massage the product into

your dog's fur. You may notice that dog shampoo doesn't lather as much as human products; this makes it easier to rinse the shampoo from your Chihuahua's coat.

Rinsing is perhaps the most important part of washing your Chihuahua—so don't rush this process! If any shampoo is left to dry on the dog's skin, it can cause itching and leave your dog with a lacklustre coat. When you think you have rinsed your dog thoroughly, you may want to rinse at least one more time, just to be sure.

If you are using a separate conditioner on your Chihuahua, this is the time to apply it. Follow the product's instructions on how long to leave the product on the coat, and again, rinse your dog. An excellent alternative to conditioner is a homemade vinegar-water rinse. Simply stir a tablespoon of white vinegar into a pint of warm water. The vinegar removes excess soap residue and helps prevent dandruff. Pour on your dog, rub into his coat, and rinse again with plain water.

Cleaning With Cornflour

In a pinch, check your pantry. Cornflour makes an excellent waterless dog shampoo and can also serve as a very effective styptic powder for stopping bleeding in an emergency.

Dry your dog thoroughly after his bath, paying special attention to the chest and underbelly.

When grooming your Chihuahua, limit the number of onlookers. Most dogs prefer not to have company while being groomed, and some dogs become agitated when handled by more than one person.

Next, dampen the washcloth and wipe your dog's face and head. You may now remove the cotton balls. Using fresh cotton balls, gently wipe the inside of each ear with the mineral oil. This will keep your Chihuahua's ears lubricated, which will help reduce the buildup of wax and dirt.

Dry your dog thoroughly, paying special attention to the chest and underbelly. Blow-drying is best, but be careful you don't burn your Chihuahua's skin. Keep your hand between the blow dryer and the dog. Blow the air in the direction of hair growth. More hair will shed after bathing when your Chihuahua is just barely dry. So brush the coat as it dries, and then once again when the dog is completely dry. For long coats use a rubber comb on the dog's fringe, furnishings, and plume.

NAIL TRIMMING

Not trimming your Chihuahua's nails can be one of the most dangerous oversights a dog owner can make. When nails are too long, they can easily catch on carpeting, clothing, or even your dog's own fur. Dewclaws, the superfluous toes placed high on most dogs' feet, are especially vulnerable to this kind of snagging. If left long, dewclaws can curl under, thus puncturing the pads like a painful ingrown toenail. If a toenail is caught and pulled completely out (a very painful event), a dog can easily dislocate a toe. Long nails will also force your Chihuahua to walk on the backs of his feet, resulting in an awkward gait and ultimately the breakdown of his feet.

Trimming a dog's toenails can be one of the most intimidating of all grooming tasks. If the nail is cut too short—at the nerve centre, which causes both pain and bleeding—your dog may forgive you, but forgiving yourself may be more difficult. Since this nerve centre (commonly called the quick or nail bed) actually recedes with each trimming, it is better to trim a small amount regularly than a large amount all at once.

Proper nail trimming isn't as difficult as it may seem, but if you find yourself repeatedly nicking that nerve centre, you might want to consider taking your Chihuahua to a professional dog groomer or your dog's veterinarian for trimmings. Your Chihuahua may overlook an occasional cut, but frequent accidents will hurt both your dog's feet and your chances of getting the dog to cooperate with future nail trimmings.

If you can hear your dog's toenails clicking when he walks, it's time for a pedicure. Trim your Chihuahua's nails every two weeks, or if you notice they are hitting the floor or curling. Dogs that take regular walks outdoors (especially on concrete or pavement) will need less frequent trimming, as the nails tend to wear down naturally on rougher surfaces.

Nail Clippers

Although there are different sizes of canine nail clippers on the market, many Chihuahua owners have found that the even smaller feline versions work best for this tiny breed. There are three basic styles of nail trimmers available for both dogs and cats—scissors-style, pliers-style, and guillotine-style. Scissors-style units operate much like a pair of manicure scissors, but with a special blade for cutting an animal's toenails. Pliers-style clippers cut from side to side. With guillotine-style clippers, you place the dog's nail through a hole in the top of the tool and squeeze the handle. The two latter styles also come with built-in stoppers to help ensure that the right amount of nail is trimmed.

Your dog should only feel pressure during a nail trim—it should never be painful.

How to Trim Your Chihuahua's Nails

If your Chihuahua tolerates nail trimming well, you might be able to trim his nails by placing the dog gently on his back in your lap. If there is any resistance, however, moving the animal to a standing position is best. This is often a two-person job, with one individual focused on holding and distracting the animal. Nail trimming is easiest on Chihuahuas with white or light-coloured nails, since the quick is more visible in these dogs.

Spread the dog's foot and inspect the areas between the toes, cleaning any dirt or debris away with a damp cloth or cotton ball. Holding the dog's foot firmly, push gently on the pad to extend the nail. Then, after locating the point at which the quick ends, snip off just the hook-like end of the nail on a 45 degree angle. If you are unsure whether you have trimmed enough, it is always better to err on the side of caution. Clip one or two nails at a time, or however many your Chihuahua will tolerate, offering short breaks in between cutting. Your dog should only feel pressure during a trim, similar to what you feel when trimming your own toenails; it should never be painful.

If you accidentally cut into the quick, promptly apply direct pressure for 10 to 15 minutes with a sterile towel soaked in cold water. You may also apply styptic powder (or a styptic pad or pencil) to help stop the bleeding. Other useful items for speeding clotting include a soft bar of soap, flour, or a wet tea bag.

You may find your Chihuahua's nails to be rather sharp after a trim. Canine nail files can be purchased to help smooth down the fresh-cut edges. You may find that regular emery boards work just fine, but it will likely take many of these to get the job done. Nail grinders (electric or battery-powered rotary tools that trim the toenail by grinding it down) are an alternative to conventional trimmers that combine the processes of trimming and filing. One of the selling points of these instruments is that they help owners avoid the quick; they also automatically cauterise wounds at higher speeds. When you are finished, reward your dog for tolerating this process with a healthy edible treat.

If your Chihuahua seems sensitive about having his feet touched, make a point of handling them more often. Lightly massage them daily

Before wetting your Chihuahua, place a cotton ball gently inside each ear.

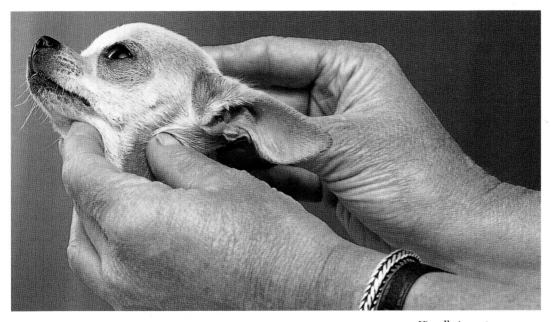

Visually inspect your Chihuahua's ears to make sure they are a healthy pink colour and free of discharge.

until it feels more natural to the dog. This will help enormously when it is once again nail-trimming time.

EAR CARE

Bath time is an excellent opportunity for ear cleaning, but it should not be the only time for this task. Unlike a human's, the canine ear canal is L-shaped, creating a moist environment that is both difficult to properly clean and especially susceptible to infection. Ear problems are uncommon in Chihuahuas due to their pricked ears that provide excellent airflow, but in order to keep your dog's ears clean and healthy, they should be cleaned weekly. Even if your Chihuahua's ears appear perfectly healthy, regular cleaning will help prevent ear mites and infection. As formerly inattentive owners can tell you, preventing these problems is much easier than treating them.

Potential Ear Problems

You will first want to visually inspect your Chihuahua's ears. Healthy ears should be a pinkish colour on the inside and free of any discharge. Next, smell the ear; it should not smell foul or strong in any way. Other symptoms of ear problems include shaking of the head or leaning to one side, pawing at the ears, swelling, redness, and sensitivity to touch.

If you discover anything out of the ordinary, don't clean the ears yourself—schedule an appointment with your Chihuahua's veterinarian. Resist the urge to clean away any discharge, as swabbing this area may be helpful to the vet in determining the cause of the problem. Remember, ear mites and infections cannot be successfully treated without the help of a veterinarian. Although you can flush the ear, this will not kill mites or cure an infection. If such a problem does exist, cleaning the ear can also irritate the skin that is likely already tender and sore. Overly zealous cleanings, even when no problem is present, can also irritate the ear lining.

Ear Hair

You might be surprised to learn that hair can grow in your Chihuahua's ear canal. You may shave or clip out this hair, as this will help keep dirt and wax from building up. Don't pull the hair. In addition to being painful, pulling can cause tiny wounds that serve as a gateway to bacteria and harmful pathogens. If hair does need to be extracted, a veterinarian should do it. Keeping your Chihuahua's ears dry will also help prevent infection, as infections flourish in moist environments.

Use a damp cloth to gently wipe sleep or tearstains out of the corners of your Chihuahua's eyes.

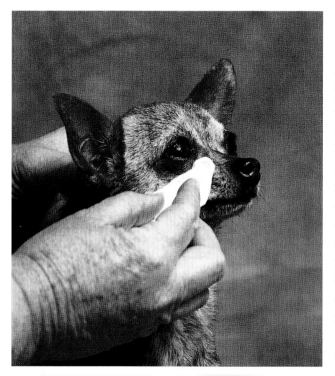

How to Clean Your Chihuahua's Ears

Ear cleaning solutions can be purchased at your pet shop or from your veterinarian. Ear cleaning wipes are also available. You may also make your own solution—a half-and-half mixture of vinegar and water. Beware of recipes including either hydrogen peroxide or isopropyl alcohol. Veterinarians discourage the use of these ingredients, as peroxide has been proven to actually eat away at the ear tissue, and even diluted alcohol can burn if merely a slight infection is present.

Squirt several drops of solution into your Chihuahua's ear.

Massage the ear downward for about 30 seconds, allowing the cleaner to penetrate any greasy dirt. Your dog will likely want to shake his head at this point. This is a good thing, as it will help loosen dirt. Next, using a cotton ball, wipe the ear from the inside out, being careful not to reach beyond the 90 degree turn that marks the end of the external ear canal and beginning of the inner ear. Also, keep in mind that ear wax does serve a function; a small amount is necessary to keep the canal properly coated.

Bad Breath Remedies

To help neutralise and prevent bad doggy breath, add a small amount of freshly chopped parsley to your Chihuahua's food. But remember, plaque and tartar are most often the culprits for foul-smelling breath, so keep brushing those teeth!

EYE CARE

Eye care is probably one of the easiest parts of grooming a Chihuahua. For many Chihuahuas, the most that has to be done is occasionally wiping a bit of sleep out of the corners of the eyes with a damp cloth. Toy breeds have very narrow tear ducts, so some owners may notice tearstains consistently forming under their Chihuahua's eyes. If this happens, you should wipe the area daily with a soft cloth dipped in distilled water. Any discharge from the eye should be clear and watery, never thick or mucous-like. Mention tearstains to your veterinarian (so an underlying cause, such as conjunctivitis, can be ruled out), but be assured that tearstains are a very common, harmless problem that is very easily remedied.

Check your Chihuahua's eyes regularly for discharge, redness, apparent itching, or squinting, as well as any changes in pupil size or reactivity. The last of these symptoms can be a sign of a serious neurological or ocular problem, and veterinary care should be sought immediately if noted.

DENTAL CARE

Like other dog breeds, Chihuahuas need regular dental care. Over the years canine dental health has evolved from simply giving your dog hard foods and biscuits as a way of reducing plaque and tartar, to actually brushing your dog's teeth with one of the many canine toothpastes available today.

Potential Dental Problems

As is the case for humans, canine dental disease isn't just a cosmetic problem. Certainly, a Chihuahua that receives regular dental care will be more attractive and have more pleasant breath, but did you know that keeping your Chihuahua's mouth clean can

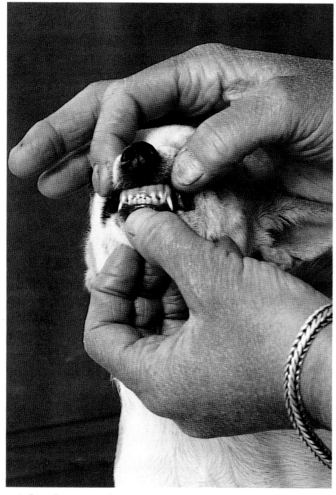

Inflamed gums may be a sign of gum disease, which can spread to the root of the tooth and eventually lead to tooth loss.

actually save his life? Bacteria from dental infections can easily enter into the bloodstream and cause significant problems to your dog's heart, liver, and kidneys.

Bad breath, inflamed gums, and tartar buildup are all signs that your dog isn't receiving proper dental care. Inflamed gums are a symptom of gum disease, also called gingivitis. A dog suffering from gingivitis is in discomfort and should be seen by a veterinarian promptly. If the gingivitis spreads to the root of the tooth, periodontal disease has set in. This can cause severe pain and even tooth loss.

As plaque accumulates on your dog's teeth, it mineralises to form tartar, a condition that can only be remedied by a professional cleaning. Unlike a trip to your own dentist for a cleaning, however, your Chihuahua will need to be anaesthetised for the procedure. Your vet will prescribe an antibiotic to clear up any infection and minimise the damage caused to internal organs before conducting the cleaning. He or she will also likely suggest pre-anaesthetic testing to help determine if your dog is a healthy candidate for anaesthesia. Both older and overweight dogs are especially vulnerable to the risks of anaesthesia. For all these reasons, it is much wiser to provide your Chihuahua with routine dental maintenance rather than trying to make up for lost time later.

The pioneers of canine dental care were correct about those hard pieces of kibble and biscuits. Dry dog food and treats that help cleanse the teeth (whether conventional canine snacks or baby carrots) are an excellent starting point for preventing plaque and tartar. Providing safe chew toys will also help keep teeth clean and sharp—and provide hours of pleasure for your Chihuahua. In order to keep your dog's mouth as clean as possible, though, you must do more than this.

Dental Supplies

Brushing should be done regularly, every day if possible. Most pet shops carry toothbrush kits, which usually include canine toothpaste, a conventional brush, and a finger toothbrush. As the name indicates, this short, flexible sheath-like instrument with soft plastic bristles fits right over the owner's finger. Many dogs tolerate this device better than the longer brush, especially older dogs that are new to brushing. There are also many different specially flavoured canine toothpastes available in such delectable varieties as beef, poultry, and seafood. You can make your own mild canine toothpaste from baking soda and water, but never use a human brand on your Chihuahua. Swallowing human toothpaste can easily make a dog sick.

How to Brush Your Chihuahua's Teeth

As with nail trimming, tooth brushing is something you may have to introduce gradually. Start with just opening your dog's mouth and touching the teeth and gums lightly with your fingertips. If your dog tolerates this, wrap your finger in a piece of wet cotton gauze and gently massage the same area. The next time add some toothpaste to the gauze (or try moving on to the finger toothbrush), and focus on the area where teeth meet the gums—the spot where tartar tends to build up the most. When done brushing, rinse your dog's teeth with a clean wet cloth or a squeeze bottle, and then offer a bowl of fresh water. Swallowing canine toothpaste or baking soda won't harm your dog, but rinsing will leave your Chihuahua's mouth feeling cleaner and more refreshed.

Tips for Evaluating a Grooming Facility

- Is the facility well lit?
- Does it look and smell clean?
- Does the staff appear knowledgeable and caring? Do they handle pets gently?
- Are cages adequately sized? Are dogs and cats caged in separate areas?
- Are pets monitored regularly to prevent overheating during blow-drying?
- Does the groomer keep complete pet records (including grooming, medical, vaccination, and emergency contact information)?

PROFESSIONAL GROOMING

Many Chihuahua owners prefer to have their dogs professionally groomed. Some lead busy lives and simply do not have time for all the tasks. Others may not feel confident in their abilities to groom their Chihuahuas as well as they would like. Whatever the reason for using a groomer's services, it is important that your Chihuahua's needs are met with care and respect.

Like many businesses, the dog grooming industry has become a large one. Chihuahua owners in virtually every part of the country can open their local yellow pages to find dozens of listings for dog groomers. Some will even come to you. These mobile groomers arrive in a fully equipped van and groom your dog on your premises while you wait. Figuring out which options are best can seem overwhelming, but by using a few guidelines, you will likely find someone with whom both you and your Chihuahua feel comfortable.

Finding a Groomer

One of the best ways to find a good groomer is also one of the easiest—word of mouth. Ask for recommendations from your breeder, veterinarian, or local breed club. If you see a well-groomed dog, ask the owner for the name of the groomer he or she uses. Although some groomers are registered or certified by their training school or professional organisation, no government agency regulates or licenses pet groomers.

Before leaving your Chihuahua with anyone, visit the facility and ask about its services, costs, and hours of operation. If you get a bad feeling, leave. If all goes well, ask for the names of some

You may want to seek help from a professional groomer for your dog, but don't neglect everyday grooming procedures as a result.

current clients that could serve as references. While a business might have a policy of not sharing their client's information with the public (a reasonable precaution for customer privacy), the company might keep a list of individuals who have offered their input for this purpose.

If your Chihuahua is seriously overdue for grooming, bringing the dog to a professional is a good idea. A professional groomer will be best at removing severe mats without any accidental cuts. Keep in mind, though, that using a groomer does not alleviate an owner from all grooming responsibility. Groomers cannot be expected to reverse long periods of inattention, so be sure to keep up with your dog's daily routine. Your Chihuahua will be very grateful.

Be clear with the groomer about your expectations. Also, be sure to inform the groomer of any health problems or other reasons why your Chihuahua might need to be handled with extra care.

Finally, when dropping your dog off for his appointment, say your goodbyes promptly. This will hopefully discourage any separation anxiety. A prolonged goodbye can leave your Chihuahua feeling apprehensive about your leaving.

Chapter

6

TRAINING AND BEHAVIOUR

of Your Chihuahua

While obedience is especially important for larger breeds, owners of toy breeds must never assume that their dogs require little or no training due to their smaller size. All dogs need to know what is expected of them. If not properly trained, a Chihuahua's behaviour problems can be just as big as those of many other dog breeds. Because this breed can be particularly stubborn, boundaries are especially important—and are much easier to establish sooner rather than later. With time and patience, your Chihuahua can be crate trained, housetrained, and learn basic obedience commands.

SOCIALISATION—WHAT, WHY, AND HOW?

One of your first and most important responsibilities of dog ownership will be properly socialising your Chihuahua. When it comes to this task, your first few weeks together are the most critical, as your puppy's temperament is still developing and extremely impressionable. During this time a dog should be exposed to as many different people as possible. This can be a catch-22, since you should also make a point of not exposing your dog to public places and all their dangers until he has finished his first year's shots, which aren't usually completed until the age of four months or older.

Since you can't bring your puppy to meet new people, the best answer is bringing people to your puppy. Entertain as many friends and family members as possible within your home during your puppy's first weeks home. Invite your guests to respectfully approach your dog, pet him, and play with him. Although you yourself are a relatively new person to your puppy, he will likely sense your ease with these people and react accordingly.

For your pup's safety, however, you must insist that before coming to your home no one visits a pet shop, dog show, or other place where strange dogs have been. There is a risk that a visitor passes a life-threatening communicable disease to your puppy. If there is any question as to a houseguest's recent activities, do not allow the person to handle your dog, and be sure to wash your floors as soon as he or she leaves, since parvovirus can exist in the ground for several years and can be carried on shoes.

If your puppy becomes accustomed to guests in his own home, he will also be more likely to accept strangers without fear or aggression when you do make your first outings to the park or other public areas. Once your dog can safely go out in public, continue socialisation exercises by taking daily walks together, bringing your dog along when you do routine errands, and participating in puppy classes. Even bringing your dog to a groomer can serve as a socialisation activity.

If your Chihuahua is no longer a puppy, it is not too late to socialise him. Although success may take more time and effort for an older dog, particularly one that has a history of abuse, it is possible if the owner is both patient and persistent. Showing your fearful Chihuahua that the world is filled with many kind people is one of the best gifts you can give your canine companion.

CRATE TRAINING

Few things seem to evoke such strong reactions among dog owners as the issue of crate training. Whether owners are for or against this training method, they are usually quite resolute in their opinions. I used to be proudly among the crate-training naysayers— thinking that keeping a dog inside what I considered a glorified

Most dogs love crates because they mimic the den environment.

Crate Accessories

Mat: For your dog's comfort, you should invest in a soft mat or another soft liner for your dog's crate. Pet shops offer a variety of choices, including faux sheepskin and covered foam. You might be tempted to use a folded blanket or towel, but you will likely find yourself having to refold these items constantly. You also want to make sure that the liner you select offers a sufficient amount of padding. Many shop-bought liners offer the ease of machine washability. You may want to purchase two liners, so your dog is never left on a cold, hard surface when one liner is being laundered.

Attachable Dishes: Most crates come with a set of dishes that mount on the inside of the crate door, but if yours does not, you might want to add them. Attachable dishes can come in handy if you have multiple dogs and wish to feed them separately. Airlines require that animals be provided with both food and water when flying long distances. Some owners also think that offering food inside his crate at home helps a dog form a positive connection with the crate.

Crate Dolly: Although your Chihuahua himself is small, carrying your dog, all his belongings, and your own luggage through a busy airport can be a demanding task. If you plan to travel with your pet, a crate dolly may be a practical investment. This is also a useful item for owners who show their dogs and attend other dog-related events with their Chihuahuas.

cage was, well, cruel. After considerable research, however, prompted by my own dog's habits, I began to change my mind.

I was in the midst of successfully training my own 12-week-old puppy when I realised that her favourite resting place when I was working was under my desk, particularly the area towards the back that was draped with the cables of various computer peripherals. Try as I may, I could not convince her that this was not the best spot in the house for a nap, and I realised that if I didn't find a solution soon, my new puppy could be in danger. I decided to try using a crate for my dog for the times that I could not prevent her from lounging under my desk, and it turned out to be one of the best choices I'd ever made.

Most dogs love crates because they mimic the den environment, and my puppy was no exception. Now an adult, she still regularly seeks out the comfort of her crate at various times throughout the day as a place to rest or just be alone. I think there are two very important reasons why my dog so readily accepted her crate. First, I never used it as a place of punishment, and second, it still allowed her to be in the same room with me while I worked (without the risk of her getting electrocuted by those dangerous cables).

A plastic crate is a more enclosed, private environment for your dog, while a wire crate provides your dog with a view of everything that's going on around him.

Crate Options

Crates come in wire or plastic versions. I opted to purchase a plastic crate for my dog, because it offered a darker, more private environment—something she seemed to be seeking. I also liked the added bonus that this option was better suited to travelling. Although airlines do not allow animals to travel in wire crates, these collapsible versions do have their advantages. If your Chihuahua prefers to feel more a part of everything going on around him, a wire crate is ideal, since your dog can see through it completely on all sides. You also always have the option of covering part of it with a blanket. While wire is more expensive than plastic, it is more resistant to damage, something to think about if your dog has a tendency towards chewing.

Introducing Your Chihuahua to the Crate

When introducing your puppy to a crate, allow some time for the dog to inspect the crate on his own. Tossing a treat inside may encourage a hesitant dog to go inside, but make sure that the door is secured in an open position, so it does not accidentally slam shut and startle the dog. If your Chihuahua enters, praise him profusely.

When your dog is repeatedly entering the crate voluntarily, start closing the door for short periods—literally just seconds at a time. Gradually increase the amount of time that passes before opening the door, ultimately leaving the room and then the house for brief periods of time until your dog is completely at ease with the routine.

Although your dog may indeed enjoy being in his crate, he should never be kept inside for more than three or four hours at a time. Even adult dogs need to empty their bladders every several hours, so if you cannot make it home to give your dog a chance to relieve himself, you must make arrangements with someone who can. Also, always give your dog a chance to empty his bladder and bowels before being crated—especially directly after eating a meal.

When Crating Is Not an Option

Not all dogs take to crating. If your Chihuahua spent a large part of his life in a crate of some sort before you got him, he may have a strong aversion to going back into one for any length of time. Adult dogs that have never been crated may also have a hard time adjusting to this very new experience. If your dog wants nothing to do with a crate, don't push. Forcing an already scared animal to do something he is adamantly against will only make matters worse.

Of course, there is nothing wrong with choosing not to give your dog a crate. Many dog owners successfully train their dogs without the use of this item, but you might want to postpone ruling it out emphatically like I did until you are certain it does not offer advantages to you and your new pet.

Chihuahuas are highly intelligent and fully capable of successful housetraining.

If you ultimately decide that a crate isn't right for your Chihuahua, I strongly recommend investing in a baby gate. This invaluable training aid may be secured into place with simple hardware that allows it to swing open whenever someone needs to walk through the doorway, or it can be attached independent of permanent fasteners, allowing the gate to be utterly portable. Many styles allow for either kind of use.

Be careful not to choose an accordion-style gate, as they present a strangulation hazard for young children. This risk could easily be transferred to a small dog. When installing any kind of gate for your dog, make sure you do not leave enough clearance at the bottom for your tiny Chihuahua to slip through (or become stuck in) during an escape attempt.

Though not as versatile as a baby gate, an exercise pen (or x-pen) also

offers the ability to keep your puppy contained in a small area until he is trained and can explore the rest of his home more safely. Resembling a wire crate missing its top and bottom, an x-pen usually consists of eight sides and a door. This is an excellent alternative for both dogs and owners with a strong objection to crating.

HOUSETRAINING

Housetraining can be one of the most distasteful aspects of dog care. If approached correctly, it can be accomplished quickly and with great pride on behalf of both dog and owner. When not readily mastered, however, it can become one of the most daunting tasks known to dog owners. It is also sadly one of the most common reasons dogs end up in shelters in need of new homes. The key to housetraining is setting yourself up for success before you even start the training process.

Whatever you do, don't fall victim to those who tell you Chihuahuas are impossible housetraining students. They're not! While it may be true that many toy dogs are not housetrained, this most often has more to do with the owners' lack of commitment than any inability on behalf of the dog. In many cases the stereotype of the toy dog doomed to failure becomes a self-fulfilling prophecy. Owners mistakenly assume that these little dogs have comparably small capabilities and lower their expectations accordingly. The truth is that like many other small dogs, Chihuahuas are highly intelligent and capable of successful housetraining (and much more!).

Dealing With Accidents

Whether you've never housetrained a puppy before or you've been doing it with relative ease throughout your life, there are a few important tips every dog owner can benefit from knowing. The most important part of effective housetraining is what you don't do. Don't yell or scold your dog for accidents. Don't hit the dog with a newspaper or any other item, including your hand. And don't rub your dog's nose in the soiled area. Although a small number of ill-informed people still believe that you must react in one of these ways when a mistake is made, the truth is that these kinds of demeaning punishments accomplish no more than frightening your dog and prolonging the desired behaviour.

Chihuahuas are believed to be difficult or even impossible to housetrain, but successful housetraining has more to do with the dedication of an owner than the breed of dog being trained.

A dog does not make the connection between your admonishments and the fact that he just urinated on the carpet. If a dog makes any connection due to your reprimand, it might be that there is something wrong about relieving himself in general. This will not encourage the dog to tell you when he has to go, but it can cause the dog to resist the urge to go even in his proper place, and lead to bladder infections and bowel obstructions.

The best thing you can do when your dog makes a mistake—and he will—is ignore it. Yes, ignore it. You shouldn't even acknowledge awareness of the accident. As soon as you notice the mistake, remove your dog from the area (crates come in handy here), and clean up the mess. You do not want your dog to witness the cleanup, though, as this could lead it to the impression that your purpose is to clean up his accidents. As soon as the mess is properly cleaned, your dog may be allowed back into the room. You should never banish a dog to his crate as a punishment for anything.

Use a product that thoroughly cleanses the area and removes odours. Several brands of effective cleaners may be purchased from pet retailers, but some dog owners insist that plain white vinegar works just as well. Even if you cannot smell anything after the cleanup, remember that your dog's nose is exponentially more

Paper Training and Crates

There is no rule stating that a paper-trained dog cannot have a crate. If you wish to provide your indoor dog with a special place of his own, there is a good chance your Chihuahua will be quite appreciative of a crate. From travelling to keeping your dog safe when you need to leave your new puppy alone for short periods of time, this versatile item will also offer you some valuable advantages.

sensitive than a human's. Dogs use scents as a way of choosing the spot on which to relieve themselves, so they will be more inclined to go in an area that has been previously soiled if they can still smell any residue. Avoid cleaning products containing ammonia, since canine urine is high in ammonia. Using these products will just encourage your dog to revisit the area for a future potty break.

When cleaning urine from carpeting, be sure to absorb the urine from the area completely before applying any cleaning agent. Paper towels work well for this purpose. Keep applying pressure to the area until you see no sign of wetness. If you apply a cleaner too early, you may be just partially masking the odour instead of removing it entirely.

Outdoor Training

Many owners choose to train their dogs to relieve themselves outdoors—either during walks or in a specific area, usually a section of a garden. No one enjoys dealing with animal excrement, but outdoor training works best for those owners who prefer not to deal with it inside their homes. It also works well for owners who are short on space, since there is no need for spread-out newspapers or litter boxes. Taking their Chihuahuas outdoors to relieve themselves also offers the added benefits of fresh air and exercise for both dogs and owners.

Using a Crate to Housetrain Your Chihuahua

As I serendipitously found with my own puppy, a crate can also be enormously useful for the purpose of housetraining. Dogs, even the youngest puppies, are naturally very clean animals. They do not wish to urinate or defecate in the same place where they sleep. By keeping your dog in a crate just large enough for him to comfortably stand up, lie down, and turn around, you eliminate the practical option of him relieving himself inside your home. When shopping for a crate, remember that bigger isn't better in this case. If the crate is too spacious, your dog might decide it has enough room to sleep at one end and relieve himself at the other.

A crate will only be an effective housetraining tool if you consistently provide your dog with opportunities to relieve himself in the appropriate place. Toy breeds need potty breaks more often than larger canines. In the beginning, your dog's schedule will be a hectic

Training your Chihuahua to relieve himself outdoors also provides him with fresh air and regular exercise.

one, but sticking to it is imperative. A two-month-old puppy needs to empty his bladder every two hours. With each additional month of age, your Chihuahua will be able to wait about another hour—with a maximum wait time of no longer than four or five hours.

Your Chihuahua will also need to empty his bowels after each meal, so take him outside shortly after he finishes eating. You should also take your dog out as soon as he wakes from napping and directly after play periods. Your dog should be placed in his crate whenever you cannot keep a close eye on him, so you can avoid as many accidents as possible.

When outside, watch your dog carefully as he inspects the area; many dogs will exhibit certain telltale signs before they relieve themselves. Circling, pacing, and sniffing are all common pre-toileting habits. If you can pinpoint your dog's warning signals, making note of them can help you avoid future accidents whenever you see your dog demonstrating these behaviours while inside the house. As soon as you witness one of these signs, immediately take your dog outside to the desired location.

When your Chihuahua relieves himself in the proper spot, praise him abundantly. If you would like to try to teach your dog to go on command, start using a specific word as soon as the dog begins relieving himself. Many dogs can be conditioned into eliminating on cue when asked to "pee" or "poop"—or whatever word or phrase you attach to each activity. Your repeated praise and the painstaking routine of taking your dog to the designated area will be the two biggest factors in successfully teaching your dog to

Patience and consistency are key elements of proper housetraining.

relieve himself outdoors. You must be patient, persistent, and vigilant, but housetraining won't last forever. Soon you will notice that more and more time has passed since your dog's last mistake.

Some dogs, particularly those who were kept in small cages during the first few weeks of life, do not respond well to the crate as a method of housetraining. Although as a breed Chihuahuas are not difficult to housetrain, dogs who spent too much of their young life in a cage may present problems. This battle can be won, but it will require extreme commitment on behalf of the owner. The good news is that once completely trained, these dogs can become every bit as reliable as any other.

Other Outdoor Housetraining Methods

If you aren't using a crate, you will need to work a little harder at housetraining. Keep your dog with you at all times during training, and be sure to stick to your dog's schedule for toileting. Since a puppy will be more likely to go whenever he feels the urge, you will have to watch him closely for the signs that the time is near.

If your dog doesn't appear to be making the connection between your chosen area and the task at hand, try taking a saturated paper towel from his last accident with you to the potty spot. The scent will encourage your dog to use this area for his bathroom business. For this reason it may also be advantageous to leave your dog's last bowel movement in the potty area as an example for your Chihuahua.

At some point in the housetraining process, a number of dogs will begin telling their owners when they have to relieve themselves. Some will scratch at the door, others will bark, and a few might even try bringing their lead to their owners. You can help the chances of your dog alerting you in this way by positioning a noise-making device near the door. A common item used by many dog owners is a string of Christmas bells.

Each time you take your dog outdoors to do his business, ring the bells (or sound whichever other device you choose), so your dog associates the noise with toileting. If your Chihuahua goes to the door and makes the sound, praise the dog and take him outside right away. He is probably trying to tell you that it's time for a potty break.

If using bells, a small amount of caution must be taken. Although bells can be an extremely helpful both during and after housetraining, a dog's claw can accidentally get caught in one of them. This could seriously injure your Chihuahua—possibly even pulling out the nail. This problem is easily prevented, though, by hanging the string securely with the bells themselves facing the door or wall.

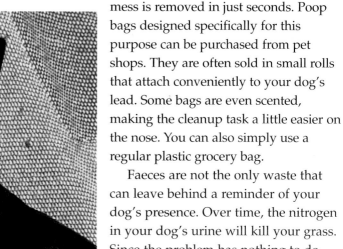

The Importance of Cleaning Up

Whether you walk your dog in public or provide him with a more private area for doing his business, cleaning up is an important part of the process. In addition to being the law on public property, cleaning up after your dog is also a basic courtesy of every dog owner. While there is certainly more freedom involved in cleaning up your own garden, the area will definitely be more pleasant if you keep it free of yesterday's faeces. In addition to being smelly and unattractive, excrement contains bacteria that can be harmful to both human and canine health.

By cleaning up after your dog promptly, you also keep abreast of any irregularities in your dog's stool that may indicate a health problem needing veterinary attention.

There are several options for the easy removal of dog wastes. Pooper-scoopers are available in a variety of sizes and designs, although carrying them along on walks is still rather impractical. These items work best for garden cleanup.

Bags are ideal in most situations. By placing a bag over your hand, you can pick up your dog's faeces and then immediately turn the bag inside out before tying it. Your hands stay clean, and the mess is removed in just seconds. Poop bags designed specifically for this purpose can be purchased from pet shops. They are often sold in small rolls that attach conveniently to your dog's lead. Some bags are even scented, making the cleanup task a little easier on the nose. You can also simply use a regular plastic grocery bag.

Faeces are not the only waste that can leave behind a reminder of your dog's presence. Over time, the nitrogen in your dog's urine will kill your grass. Since the problem has nothing to do with acid, dietary supplements that alter the pH of your dog's urine will do nothing to prevent this from occurring. The best way to prevent extensive damage is to limit your dog to one small area of the garden for toileting.

Training your dog to toilet in a certain place indoors allows him to relieve himself whenever he needs to, without you there.

Otherwise, your lawn will be sporadically spotted with brown spots of dead grass.

Indoor Training

Indoor training offers one major advantage over outdoor training—your dog can relieve himself whenever the need arises, whether anyone is home or not. This may be a considerable asset to you if you work outside the home. Many Chihuahua owners also choose this route because it is more convenient for their individual lifestyles. People who live in flats (often complete with several flights of stairs), elderly dog owners, and those who reside in colder climates all have good reasons for preferring indoor housetraining.

A Breath of Fresh Air

Though a small dog like the Chihuahua can be trained to relieve himself indoors, you should still give him frequent opportunities to go outside to get some exercise (or just a change of scenery).

Choosing the Proper Surface

The first decision you will have to make when training indoors is the surface on which your Chihuahua will relieve himself. Newspapers are a common choice, since they are both convenient and inexpensive. Some owners, however, prefer a litter box. Although this option is more expensive than newspaper, it is fairly easy to clean and generally more attractive. Both methods are equally effective.

Dog litter may sound like a new-fangled word used merely to charge a higher price for an old item (cat litter), but there are legitimately important differences between the two mediums. Dog litter is larger than its feline counterpart and also more absorbent. Many dogs also have an inexplicable tendency to eat kitty litter, and this can be harmful to your dog's health. To give you an idea as to how much you would spend on dog litter, a 12-pound (5.4 kg) bag should last the average toy dog approximately three to four weeks. Depending on your litter—and newspaper—of choice, the difference in cost (after the initial litter box purchase) may be minimal.

Although few things may seem more difficult than properly balancing a puddle of urine on a piece of newspaper while disposing of it, the more manageable choice of canine litter boxes do come with a certain amount of necessary housekeeping. In order to keep your dog's litter box smelling fresh and clean, you will not only need to change the litter itself, but you will also need to give the entire unit a thorough cleaning about once a week. This will keep the box more pleasant for both your dog and the rest of the household.

Many people choose newspaper for indoor housetraining.

How to Housetrain Indoors

Not surprisingly, indoor training is very similar to outdoor training. You will still need to establish a schedule for your puppy and bring him to his paper or litter box frequently. Place your dog on the papers at all the same times—following meals, after naps or periods of play, etc. When your Chihuahua goes on the paper, praise him delightedly. When he relieves himself in unacceptable spot, remove the dog from the room temporarily while you clean up the mishap entirely, and then continue with the training schedule.

While you don't want to leave several urine-soaked areas of newspaper on your floor, do leave one wet paper when cleaning up your dog's successes. Place this piece just underneath the top layer of fresh paper, as a way of reminding your Chihuahua of the purpose of the newspaper. (Once your dog is fully housetrained, you will be able to do away with this step.)

Transitional Methods

While you shouldn't expect your Chihuahua to repeatedly toggle between indoor and outdoor housetraining, there might be situations in which a transition is warranted. Perhaps you will move to an apartment or flat where the policy states that all dogs need to go outdoors. Or maybe your older dog cannot manage the cold as well as when he was younger. In some cases, illness (either your own or your dog's) makes a transition to indoor toileting necessary. Whatever the circumstances, a transition can be possible, but it will likely take both time and effort.

Indoors to Outdoors

In some cases owners prefer to begin housetraining indoors and then move towards outdoor toileting as the puppy attains some success with newspapers. The theory here is often that younger dogs will likely be more adaptable to the transition. While this may indeed be true, it is still a less than ideal way of teaching a puppy your expectations. If you are certain from the beginning that you want your Chihuahua to relieve himself outdoors, it is far better to begin using this method of training at the beginning.

If you need to train your indoor dog to relieve himself outside, the best way to start is bringing the indoor potty out with you. Whether your Chihuahua uses a litter box or newspapers, taking either item outdoors will help show your dog that the protocol is changing. Before starting the transition, take note of your dog's schedule of indoor toileting, and begin taking your dog outdoors just before those times. As with your original training, praise your dog effusively whenever he goes outdoors. Eventually, you will be able to do away with the box or newspapers, but wait until your dog has mastered the task of using it in his new location.

Outdoors to Indoors

Transitioning a dog from outdoor toileting to using papers or a litter box may prove a bit more difficult than the other way around, but it is possible if an owner is patient and plans ahead. Begin by bringing a small part of the new method outside with you when your dog goes out to relieve himself. Place a newspaper or a handful of litter on your dog's regular potty spot immediately upon reaching his outdoor potty spot. Encourage your dog to go as you normally would, but on the new item. As with all forms of training, praise your Chihuahua intensely when he does as you ask.

Transitioning your dog from toileting outside to inside (or vice versa) will take time and effort.

Once your dog has achieved some success with going on the paper or litter outdoors, introduce the litter box by placing it outside beside the outdoor potty area, and then begin encouraging the dog to go inside the box. As your dog becomes more and more comfortable with using the indoor paraphernalia, start gradually moving the papers or box away from the outdoor spot and closer to your home. The ultimate change will be moving the items indoors, where you will still continue instructing your dog when it is time for toileting.

When Accidents Indicate a Bigger Problem

Health Issues

Occasionally a previously well-trained dog will begin relieving himself in inappropriate places. If your dog suddenly begins

When training outdoors, keep your Chihuahua safe by making sure you're in a fenced-in area.

having accidents, the first thing you should do is contact your veterinarian. Incontinence is a symptom of many health problems, including kidney problems and diabetes. Your vet will need to rule these conditions out before suggesting a plan of action to remedy the housetraining setback.

Dogs are extremely sensitive to dietary changes. Any sudden change can cause digestive upset. This can result in diarrhoea or, occasionally, temporary loss of bowel control. If your Chihuahua has eaten something that didn't agree with him, he may not be able to make it to the appropriate toileting area in time. Do not scold the dog for this. Remedial housetraining also shouldn't be necessary following an isolated incident. If the problem is ongoing, however, you should have your dog checked by his vet.

Discovering blood in your dog's stool can be frightening, but chances are very good that the problem isn't as bad as you fear. Although in humans this is often a sign of serious illness, bloody stool is surprisingly more common in dogs. It does, however, signal a problem, so a veterinary exam should be scheduled. Your vet can determine if your dog is suffering from a parasite, an infection, or perhaps a more serious condition such as colitis. Oftentimes bleeding is a result of a foreign object (such as a piece of bone) that has scraped the inside of your dog's large intestine.

Whether your dog is trained to defecate indoors or outdoors, regularly check your dog's stool during the cleanup process. This can alert you to a health problem as early as possible. Contact your vet if your dog has passed bloody stools, dark, tarry-looking stools, or stools containing visible worms or other parasites. You will likely be asked to bring a stool sample, which you can carry to the vet's office in a ziplock bag.

Blood in urine is also a cause for concern and warrants a trip to the veterinarian. Although pink or red-tinged urine is usually a sign of a bladder infection, it can also be a symptom of a more serious problem, such as bladder cancer. This is a case in which having an accident indoors could be a blessing, since owners who walk their dogs may never have noticed the blood otherwise. If possible, bring a urine sample with you to the vet. This should be a free-catch sample, which means it is collected in a small container (a clean baby food jar, for instance) directly as the Chihuahua urinates. Although this may sound difficult, another symptom of a bladder infection is frequent urination often accompanied by great urgency; so another opportunity to collect a sample should present itself rather soon.

Submissive Urination and Marking

Be careful you don't confuse submissive wetting or excitable wetting with intentional urination, as these are not housetraining issues. Some dogs tend to leak urine at certain times, such as when their owners arrive home. Often they will lie down exposing their bellies in the process. This is done to show the owner that the dog knows his place in the pack and that he sees the owner as a superior dog.

If your housetrained Chihuahua suddenly begins having accidents, a trip to the vet is in order.

Like people, dogs are in many ways only as old as they feel. It is up to owners to make sure their dogs' lives remain stimulating and filled with opportunity for ongoing learning. Play and exercise should be a part of every dog's life. An older dog might be more set in his ways than a new puppy, but dogs generally never lose their curiosity, a major motivator for continued learning.

You can minimise these kinds of accidents by ignoring your Chihuahua whenever you enter the home. Although it may seem harsh, avoiding an immediate greeting will help your dog retain control of his bladder. When you do greet your dog, avoid high-pitched tones, as they can elicit overexcitement. Also, avoid being too loud with both your voice and your movements, since either can draw out submissive behaviours. Never scold a dog for these kinds of accidents. In the case of submissive wetting, it can actually make the problem worse.

Marking behaviour, urinating done for the sake of identifying territory with scent, can be discouraged in a few ways. First, have your dog spayed or neutered. Although this may not solve the problem entirely, it will reduce your Chihuahua's urge to mark territory significantly. Remember, the cost of spaying or neutering is less than having your carpets cleaned just once. Second, thoroughly clean the areas your dog has marked. Third, begin the housetraining process again. Finally, if the problem still persists, consider taking your dog for obedience training. This can help your dog accept his position under the others in the household and discourage him from focusing on marking his turf.

BASIC OBEDIENCE

Some Chihuahua owners may balk at the term obedience training. Certainly they can see the necessity of formally training a Newfoundland or German Shepherd, but they fail to see the benefits of traditional training for smaller breeds like their own. Every dog deserves to be taken seriously, and this means expecting the same level of behaviour from your Chihuahua as you would from any other canine. Defiant behaviour should never be rationalised because you think your dog is too little to understand or too small to be a legitimate threat. You also cannot blame your dog for poor behaviour. Proper behaviour must be taught, and teaching it is the owner's responsibility.

Bad behaviour is also taught, although it has the potential of becoming even more deeply ingrained, since owners are often not even aware of its occurrence. Whenever you tolerate bad behaviour from your dog, you teach the animal that his actions are acceptable. You would never allow your three-year-old daughter to defy you without correcting her and making your expectations clear, but for some reason many owners think it is harmless to be passive with their small-breed dogs, even those long past the puppy stage.

In order to explain what basic obedience is, you must first understand what it isn't. Basic obedience is not about teaching your Chihuahua to perform tricks. It is also not about turning your dog into a quiet robot bereft of personality and zeal. With proper training your dog should retain all the qualities of his unique character while developing a clear understanding of your expectations as his owner.

If you plan to involve your dog in obedience competitions, your goals will be more extensive than that of the typical companion dog owner. Basic obedience (what every dog should know and a starting ground for all dogs) consists of teaching simple commands that may be used on a daily basis (such as heel, sit, down, stay, and come). Perhaps even more important than the commands themselves is the foundation you are building for your dog to meet your expectations by following these commands. You are essentially teaching your dog how to listen to and obey you. You are also building trust between dog and owner.

Obedience is best learned from a qualified instructor in a

Training your Chihuahua will help build trust and confidence.

comfortable setting for both you and your dog. The process should be structured yet fun and centred around positive methods of training. You can certainly work on basic commands within the privacy of your own home or garden, but bringing your dog to an obedience class offers you the added benefits of an expert's instruction and advice and offers your dog the added benefit of socialisation.

Beware of training methods that include any type of punishment. Your dog should be praised for successfully completing a task, but never reprimanded for failure. Effective dog training is about gentle instruction, continuous patience, and abundant praise.

Finding a Trainer

Finding a trainer may be an easy task, but selecting the right one can prove a bit more difficult. There are almost as many different styles of training as there are trainers, and unfortunately no licensing is currently required to work in this field. This makes it even more important for dog owners to be sure they are dealing with a reputable trainer who uses humane methods.

Your veterinarian and local animal shelter are two of the best resources for reliable referrals. Your breeder may be even better able to point you towards a good trainer who has experience with Chihuahuas. You may also contact the Association of Pet Dog Trainers (APDT) at www.apdt.co.uk for the name of a trainer in your area. The APDT does have a certification process for its trainers. Since such a huge part of a trainer's job involves instructing the owner, it is extremely important that the two of you have a good rapport. You will also want someone with a broad knowledge of canine health and behaviour.

The trainer should provide you with clear instructions for every lesson and demonstrate the techniques before you are given the opportunity to practice them with your dog. Health precautions such as vaccination requirements should be prerequisites for attendance in group settings. Class sizes should be limited so there is ample time for individual questions and feedback. Beware of any trainer who offers you a guarantee for results, as every dog is different and will learn at a different pace.

A trainer will be little help to you if you don't have a clear idea of your goals for your dog. If your dog has a problem with excessive barking at strangers, for instance, you need to talk to your trainer about the best methods of correcting this behaviour. Training will also demand that you follow through with the methods you are taught. If you only perform the exercises during class and don't reinforce them with practice at home, you will likely never succeed at improving your dog's behaviour.

Most of all, training should be fun for both you and your dog. A positive approach is not only more enjoyable for you both, but it also produces better results. Punishing your dog by yelling, hitting, jerking his lead, or isolating him will only decrease your dog's motivation—and hurt your

You may want to seek out the help of a professional when training your dog.

relationship with the animal. Completely ignoring a failed attempt is far more effective, since what your Chihuahua wants most is your praise. Accordingly, always end on a positive note, so your dog can feel a sense of accomplishment and be more likely to return to his next training session with the best possible attitude towards future learning.

Training Using Food Rewards

One of the best and most positive ways to train your Chihuahua is using food or praise as a reward when he exhibits a desired behaviour. Many trainers use this type of reward-based method that reinforces positive behaviours and avoids using punishment as a motivator. Some dogs respond to praise, but most dog owners find that food is universally a primary motivator when it comes to dogs. The treats used as a reward should be extremely tiny, so your Chihuahua doesn't fill up too quickly during the training sessions, and can consist of anything your dog finds tasty—cut up pieces of hot dog, cheese, chicken, etc.

To use this method of training, use a positive tone of voice to praise your Chihuahua as soon as he performs a particular command, while simultaneously offering a treat. Timing is crucial with this type of training, so it can be helpful to have a professional trainer show you the ropes.

As your dog begins to show some success, continue to offer

In order for training to work, the entire family must follow through with the training methods at home.

praise each time a task is performed, but offer the food reward more sporadically. Food rewards should be gradually phased out as new tasks are mastered. You may want to return to food rewards, however, whenever you introduce a new command.

The more verbal praise you offer alongside the edible rewards, the easier time you will have eliminating the food. Never cease to praise your dog when he follows your commands. Although treats help to hold your dog's attention and reinforce success, a dog's biggest reward is knowing his master is pleased with a job well done.

Always train your dog before he has eaten. This way your dog will be more interested in earning the reward, and you will be able to adjust the portion of his next meal accordingly. If your dog is no longer a puppy and is already carrying some extra weight, you will need to be especially vigilant. Generally dogs that respond best to food rewards are ones that aren't overfed at other times.

Clicker Training

First used in the 1940s, clicker training is considered by many dog owners to be a more relaxed and fun approach than traditional command-based training. It is based on a proven scientific method of learning called operant conditioning. By marking a desired behaviour the instant it occurs with a two-toned clicking sound

Canine Body Language

Elbows Lowered With Bottom in the Air

Often referred to as the play-bow, this most adorable stance that usually includes tail wagging and a good-natured bark is an invitation for play. Your Chihuahua may use this gesture with his human family members or other animals within the home.

Exposed Belly

To show his submissive position, a dog will lie on his back and raise one leg when a dominant member of the pack arrives. With his ears back and belly exposed, this dog is telling you he is not a threat.

Sleeping on His Back

While your Chihuahua's exposed belly indicates submission when your dog is awake, a dog lying this way before going to sleep is essentially telling you he doesn't have a care in the world. Since lying on his back this way leaves him extremely vulnerable, only a dog who feels completely secure will sleep in this position.

Ears Forward or Back, Tail Straight Up, Teeth Exposed

With or without the teeth exposed, this is an aggressive posture. It also may or may not be accompanied by growling, loud barking, or even snapping. An angry dog will usually hold eye contact challengingly.

Ears Down, Tail Hanging Limp

A dog lying in this position is bored. Perhaps it's time to break out the squeaky toys.

Cowering or Hiding Behind Furniture

If your dog is frightened, he may hide behind or beneath a chair or other piece of furniture. This springs from your dog's natural instinct to seek the safety of his den when danger is present.

from a small plastic device dubbed a clicker, the trainer reinforces the behaviour instantaneously with the sound and then rewards it with a treat. As with other styles of positive training, punishment for failure is never used with clicker training.

What separates clicker training most from other forms of conditioning-based training is the timing of the click. Rewards, such as edible treats or praise, are offered directly after a desired behaviour, whereas the clicking sound must be made during the desired behaviour. Although your dog may initially get distracted by the click and discontinue the behaviour, the timing of the sound is paramount. The timing of the treat—all-important in reward-based training—is far less important.

One of the biggest advantages to clicker training is that it helps you catch your dog doing the things you want repeated. The theory is that in time, your dog will begin showing you the desired behaviours on his own, expecting the click. At this time you should begin offering a cue for your Chihuahua to connect with each

Involving the Whole Family

Unfortunately, what you and your dog accomplish together over several weeks can be undone in just a matter of days if another family member isn't aware of the new protocol. Encourage all members of the household to participate in the dog's training. Ask your trainer how many people may attend classes with your Chihuahua. Although space can sometimes make it necessary to limit the number of human participants, most trainers will encourage the attendance of as many family members as possible.

If only one person is responsible for your Chihuahua's training, it is quite possible that he or she will become the only one the Chihuahua obeys or seeks out in times of need. Because Chihuahuas tend to bond so closely with just one family member, it is especially important that your dog understands that he does not directly follow you in the family hierarchy. When you cannot be there to care for your dog, he must treat others with respect and not as his servants.

Even children can be part of the programme. Involving your kids in the training process can help your Chihuahua see them as family members who deserve his love and respect. It also presents the perfect opportunity to teach younger children how to properly treat a small dog. Education is contagious. When taught the right ways, your kids will also be very likely to pass on their knowledge about animal care to the children of friends and relatives who regularly visit your household.

behaviour. When the dog responds to the cue, you can then offer the click followed by a reward, but only if the behaviour happens during or after the cue. So, even though this regimen doesn't focus on commands, you will still be able to train your dog to respond to your instructions.

Another important rule of clicker training is only clicking once (pushing in, then releasing) for every time your dog demonstrates a particular behaviour. It is fine to click for a behaviour that is only a step towards the final goal, though. This is actually the best way to move your dog closer to your objectives. Eventually, as each behaviour is mastered, you will discontinue using the clicker for that task, and begin using it for a new one.

Clicker training is not rocket science, but it is a science—so an instructor can be extremely helpful in showing you the best ways to use this effective technique. Although it may seem counterproductive for a large group of people to gather and make clicking noises all at once, a dog's hearing is so much better than our own that they are surprisingly capable of discerning their owner's click from any other. Classes are offered in many areas for this kind of dog training.

TEACHING BASIC OBEDIENCE

Teaching your dog to respond to any of these commands can take time. Whenever training an animal, your patience and persistence are your most important tools. If you are working with

a rescued dog who appears to display a negative reaction to a particular word (possibly due to past abuse), you can certainly use another word (such as "here" instead of "come") in its place. The important things are that you are consistent with whichever term you choose and that you always use a pleasant tone.

Because Chihuahuas can be stubborn, training them can be a bit more difficult than a more amenable breed, such as a Labrador Retriever. Fortunately, what a Chihuahua lacks in compliance he makes up for in intelligence. With consistent yet gentle training, most Chihuahuas learn commands relatively quickly if owners start the training process when their dogs are young.

Bear in mind that short, frequent training sessions will yield better results than an entire Saturday morning spent teaching commands. Begin working with your puppy in five-minute sessions three times a day. As your Chihuahua matures, you can gradually increase the length to 10 minutes, then to 15 by around eight months of age.

Come

While it may not be paramount that your Chihuahua learns the full gamut of obedience commands, consider the value of at least one—*come*. If your Chihuahua should ever escape the safety of your home, having taught him just this one command could literally save his life.

You may think your faithful dog would never run away from you and into a street of moving vehicles, but it happens to dogs just like yours every day. Housedogs in particular have no idea how to react when faced with the reality of being outside without a lead or harness. Oftentimes they panic and bolt.

Begin introducing this command to your Chihuahua as soon as you bring the dog home. Whenever you catch your puppy in the midst of running to you on his own, say the word "come" immediately, and then bestow him with an enthusiastic greeting as a reward. Practice this command frequently for the first few months of your dog's life, and continue it periodically thereafter.

Once you familiarise your Chihuahua with the command, begin using it while your dog is outside on his lead. Allow the dog to walk away from you a bit (extendable leads serve this purpose extremely well), and then say the word "come" in an upbeat and welcoming tone. Shower the dog with praise when he complies. If

Always the Chased, Never the Chaser

One of the biggest mistakes an owner can make is chasing his or her dog during play. By doing so you are essentially teaching your dog to run away from you. This does not mean you must decline if your dog initiates a thrilling game of chase. Just make sure that you are always the one being chased, and that the game remains playful and fun. Through well-planned playtime, you will be training your dog to always follow you.

If your Chihuahua knows the come command you will be able to retrieve him if he ever escapes from home.

your Chihuahua does not come to you, pull the lead gently towards you while never changing the happy tone of your voice as you repeat the command. Be sure to praise the dog as soon as he reaches you. Because you may need to pull lightly on your dog's lead during this exercise, it is recommended that you use a harness instead of a collar during each training session to prevent your Chihuahua's delicate neck from being injured. It is imperative that you never practice this exercise when your dog is off his lead. Even if you are both within an enclosed area, you must have a means of making the dog follow your command. If you prefer not to use a lead, have a friend walk your dog to you when you issue the command if he doesn't swiftly come on his own. The person should physically guide the animal by his midsection, with no greater force than you would pull on a lead.

You must never scold your dog when he comes to you. There may be times you find this rule a difficult one, but it is vital that you remember it—even if your dog has done something extremely naughty. Your dog must never fear coming to you.

Sit

The *sit* command is the basis for many others, so it is a wonderful starting point for all future training. Even the youngest puppies are often capable of learning it. Holding a treat in your closed hand, place the hand just above your dog's nose. As your dog moves his snout towards the treat, lift your hand slightly up and over your dog's head. This will naturally encourage your dog to shift his weight onto his haunches, moving himself into the sitting position. Once your dog sits, open your hand and offer the treat.

You should practice this command often and in a variety of places, so your dog is accustomed to sitting whenever and wherever you say the word. Be sure to spend at least some time working near the main entrance of your home, though, as this will make it easier to get your dog to comply even with the excitement of a visitor's arrival.

Down

The *down* command follows the *sit* command. It can be especially useful for helping your dog stay out of trouble, particularly when a person or another dog is approaching.

Beginning with your Chihuahua in a sitting position, hold a treat in front of your dog, and then slowly lower your hand in front of his paws as you say the word "down." When your dog lowers his body to get the treat, offer both the treat and verbal praise. Teaching this command can be difficult with a Chihuahua, since there is such a small amount of space to begin with between the dog and the floor. If lowering your hand does not work, instead try slowly pulling the treat forward. This can also draw your dog downward.

Once your dog is easily moving into the down position as a response to your moving hand, start issuing the *down* command just before you show your dog the treat, and begin gradually limiting how far you lower or extend your hand. This will help wean your dog from depending on the visual cue.

Stay

Successfully learning the *stay* command can actually save your dog's life. For example, using this command whenever your

"Sit" is a wonderful starting command—even the youngest of puppies are capable of learning it.

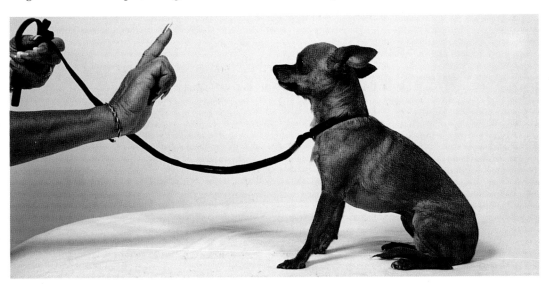

"But I Only Want a Housedog"

Some dog owners prefer not to go the route of extensive training. They may simply not care whether their Chihuahuas sit on command, or they might mistakenly assume there is no practical reason that their indoor dogs learn to heel upon command. They may think that training is a waste of time and money for them. Remember that Chihuahuas are extremely intelligent beings who are learning all the time, whether you are deliberately teaching them or not. Training teaches dogs the rules; without it they are forced to make up their own.

Whether you want to teach your Chihuahua a few simple commands or you decide to seek the help of a professional trainer for a more formal programme, as the dog's owner, you should be actively involved in the training process. If you simply send your dog to a training programme, the dog may respond well to the trainer but return home unwilling to obey the same commands when spoken by you.

doorbell rings can prevent your dog from running out the door when it opens. *Stay* can also be helpful when entertaining a visitor who is uncomfortable around dogs.

Once your dog can reliably sit when told, you can begin working on the stay command. Expect puppies to only remain still for just a second or two at first, but this duration will increase over time.

After instructing your pup to sit, raise your hand in a stop-sign gesture while saying the word "stay." Take a step back, and then return to your dog, providing a treat and praise. Make sure your dog does not stand or move as you present the treat, as this will reward the wrong behaviour.

When your dog is able to sit for a few seconds, begin gradually increasing both the number of steps you take away from the dog and the amount of time before offering the reward. Your ultimate goal is for your dog to remain sitting and still for about a minute or longer with you at least ten feet away.

Drop It/Leave It

The *drop it* and *leave it* commands can protect your dog from any number of dangers, including choking and being poisoned. *Drop it* can also be helpful when playing fetch.

Begin teaching the *drop it* command using your Chihuahua's favourite toys, since you will want your dog to obey no matter how appealing the item in question may be. Give the toy to your dog, allowing him to play with it for a few minutes, and then say "drop it." As you issue the command, gently remove the item from your dog's mouth. Praise your Chihuahua as soon as he lets go of the item. You may then return the toy to your dog and allow him to play with it a few more minutes before repeating the exercise. Eventually, your dog will relinquish the item when the command is issued without any physical prompting. At this point, you should move on to using other toys or bones, so your Chihuahua isn't left with the notion that he must only surrender this one item when the *drop it* command is issued.

Though similar to *drop it*, the *leave it* command works a little differently, as you don't want your dog to touch the item in question in this situation. With your Chihuahua's lead on, allow your dog to play with one of his toys for a few minutes. Then, toss another favourite plaything into your dog's view. If your dog's attention is averted towards the new item, as it will likely be, issue

Even though you can carry a Chihuahua almost anywhere, your dog should still learn to walk properly on a lead.

the *leave it* command as soon as your dog moves towards the new item. At first you will need to use the lead to keep your Chihuahua from the item, but as soon as you are able to interrupt the natural tendency to investigate the new item with just the command, reward your dog for responding as desired. Once your Chihuahua learns the command, you should then practice the exercise without the lead.

Walking on a Lead

Part of this breed's appeal is obviously its portability. You may want to carry your dog with you nearly every place you go—and this is fine, but don't overlook the value of lead training. Chihuahuas, like all other dogs, should be at ease walking on a lead. They shouldn't be fearful of it or pull while taking walks.

The best way to acclimate your dog to his lead is by making it a part of his daily routine. Leave your Chihuahua's lead where he can sniff it over and become

Chihuahuas are not particularly prone to problem behaviours, but their natural stubbornness can make them more difficult to correct.

acquainted with it. Within the safety of your home, allow your dog to wear the lead for gradually increased periods of time until he seems comfortable with it. Be careful, of course, that the lead doesn't get caught on anything inside the home, and keep your dog away from stairs—don't allow the dog out of your sight. Praise your dog elaborately whenever he tolerates the lead. If you use food rewards, bestow the dog with a treat along with this heartfelt praise.

Eventually, begin taking your Chihuahua outdoors on the lead, continuing to praise him as you walk around together. Keep the training sessions short—just a few minutes each day. Ultimately, you will begin putting just a bit of pressure on the lead as you lead your dog in one direction or another. It is vitally important that you are gentle and that your dog does not pull. Offer treats as your dog is in the process of walking along and never when he is resisting the lead.

Heel

The *heel* command instructs your dog to walk along with you in sync with your pace and sit on his own accord whenever you stop. Though most often used in obedience trials, this command can be helpful to all dog owners who walk their dogs on leads.

Teaching the *heel* command can take some time. First, your dog needs to learn how to walk on a lead without pulling. This is a good beginning task for younger puppies, since they are often too young to fully grasp the *heel* command. Second, great care needs to be taken not to yank or pull too hard on your Chihuahua when keeping him in line with both your direction and pace.

Begin walking your dog on your left side with the lead secured in your right hand; your left hand can then be used to pick up slack when needed. Hold a treat in your left hand, instruct the dog to sit, and praise him for complying. Next, say the word "heel" in an upbeat tone, and begin walking briskly for a few paces. When you stop, lift the lead up a bit so that your dog sits, and offer the reward along with more praise.

PROBLEM BEHAVIOURS

Problem behaviours such as digging, chewing, excessive barking, and aggression are more than just unpleasant. They can lead to the harsh reality of disgruntled neighbours and landlords, financial reimbursement for destroyed items, and the owner's frustration and anxiety over these issues. Many owners dealing with these problems feel pulled in several directions. They love their dogs and want desperately for them to stop these destructive behaviours, and they feel the pressure of others' expectations, but they just don't know how to change them.

Are Chihuahuas more prone to problem behaviours than other dogs? Not really. Like other breeds, Chihuahuas possess tendencies toward both positive and negative traits. It is vital to remember that these qualities (both good and bad) are not inevitable, nor is any particular characteristic present in every dog. Generally Chihuahuas are very stubborn, so this makes correcting bad behaviour a greater challenge than for many other breeds. Consistency in training is a must for these small dogs with definite minds of their own.

Ten Tips for Preventing Behaviour Problems

1. Set rules immediately and stick to them.
2. Avoid situations that promote inappropriate behaviour.
3. Observe the pet and provide what he needs to be cared for and attended to.
4. Supervise the new pet diligently through undivided individual attention and training, and restrict the pet's access to a limited area of the house until training is complete.
5. Encourage good behaviour with praise and attention.
6. Correct bad behaviours by providing positive alternatives—trading a toy for a slipper, for example.
7. Never physically punish or force compliance to commands. This may lead to fear biting or aggression.
8. Don't play rough or encourage aggression or play biting.
9. Expose pets to people, animals, and environments where you want them to live.
10. See your veterinarian if serious or unresolved behaviour problems exist.
    (Courtesy of the AAHA)

Inappropriate Chewing

There are many possible reasons behind inappropriate chewing. Teething, anxiety, boredom, and lack of exercise are all potential causes. To avert your dog from using your personal property as chew toys, provide him with a variety of acceptable items for chewing. Toys that present the opportunity for stimulation, such as balls that release treats upon manipulation, can also be helpful in distracting your dog from feasting on your belongings.

Use the drop it command whenever you catch your dog chewing anything unacceptable. Avoid the temptation to give your dog an item he has already damaged. Although you may have no further use for it, allowing your Chihuahua to keep it will only further confuse the dog as to what is and isn't fair game. For this reason, also avoid giving your dog old shoes or clothing as toys. When your dog begins chewing an improper item, remove it from his possession, and offer one of his own chew toys as a replacement. Praise the dog if he accepts the substitute.

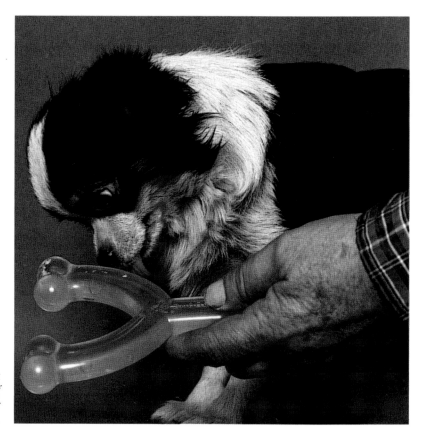

Provide your Chihuahua with a variety of acceptable items for chewing.

Chihuahuas are known for alerting their owners to the presence of strangers—socialisation can help avert problem barking.

Excessive Barking or Howling

The best method for reducing excessive barking is good old-fashioned distraction. Music can serve as a wonderful buffer if noises tend to prompt your Chihuahua's barking. Placing your dog's crate away from outside walls or windows where people and other sounds can easily be heard can also help. Socialising your dog may help if he barks mostly when you entertain visitors within your home. In this case providing your dog with a special treat that he receives only when visitors are present may be effective.

Chihuahuas are known for alerting their owners to the presence of strangers, so this may be the key factor in your dog's barking problem. You will not be able to completely stop your dog from barking when he hears a suspicious noise—and you may actually want your dog to serve this watchdog role. This doesn't mean that you want prolonged barking. In this case you should teach your dog the enough command.

In order to teach this command, you must first teach the speak command. You can do this by issuing the command as you knock on any hard surface, hopefully encouraging your dog to bark in response to the noise. Once your Chihuahua learns to speak upon command, begin implementing the word "enough" as soon as there is a break in the barking, rewarding the dog immediately for stopping. The timing of the command is crucial, as you want to issue the command as soon as your dog stops barking; otherwise you will be rewarding the wrong behaviour.

When your Chihuahua informs you of an approaching visitor or other noise, praise him for bringing the sound to your attention. Once you acknowledge the situation, say, "Enough". As soon as your dog stops barking, offer a reward. This will ultimately teach him that bringing a noise to your attention is acceptable, but continued barking is not.

Separation Anxiety

Saying Goodbye

When you have to leave your dog for a while, don't make a big production of saying goodbye, as this actually can contribute to separation anxiety.

Howling or extended barking when your dog is left at home alone can be a trickier problem. Domestic dogs often howl only when prompted by a specific sound (such as a siren), but in the wild dogs howl as means of bringing the pack together. If excessive howling or barking only occurs when your dog is left alone, this may signal the deeper problem of separation anxiety. If ignored, separation anxiety can manifest itself in the form of chewing, housetraining regression, and sometimes even self-mutilation. One indication that you are dealing with an issue of separation is if you offer your dog a treat when you leave and frequently return to see that it has remained uneaten.

The most common underlying causes of canine separation anxiety are confusion, fear, and stress. A variety of issues could be at the root of the problem. Perhaps your dog was taken from his mother too early. Maybe your dog's previous owner abandoned him at a shelter, leaving him especially fearful of your leaving him now. Maybe you have returned to working full time after taking a few weeks off to spend with your new puppy. Again, this is a situation in which teaching basic obedience skills can help your dog become a more confident, less anxious being—the key to reversing this condition.

Spend time together with your dog regularly. Take your dog for walks often; regular exercise can significantly reduce your dog's stress. Provide your dog with a crate for security, and follow the protocol of slowly introducing it while you are at home. If you cannot seem to correct the problem, consider enrolling your dog in daycare, or have someone else take care of your dog when you cannot be there. Even having a dog walker stop by midday may offer just enough of a break from the solitude to help your dog cope

with being alone while you are away. If the problem continues, seek the help of a certified animal behaviourist who has experience with this type of problem.

Chihuahuas should never be allowed to bite—even in play. It could lead to problem behaviours later in his life.

Aggression

Canine aggression must never be tolerated. Although many factors can contribute to a dog's tendency to bite, there are no acceptable excuses. If there is only one situation for which obedience training is necessary, this is it. From their very first human experiences, puppies should never be allowed to bite—not even playfully. Teaching your dog that you are his leader is the most important step in correcting aggressive behaviour. If your dog is biting, it may also be wise to consider details such as where your dog sleeps, when he is fed, and what games you play with your dog—and how these things may be affecting your dog's perception of his place in the family.

If your Chihuahua has assumed the alpha role in your household and uses aggressive behaviour toward family members as a means of retaining this position, this is a true emergency. Consult your veterinarian, a canine obedience instructor or dog trainer, or an animal behaviourist immediately for advice on how to solve this very serious problem. The fact that your Chihuahua only weighs a few pounds (kg) does not mean he is incapable of hurting someone, and you could be faced with a lawsuit, or worse, the unimaginable possibility of being legally forced to euthanise your dog.

Getting Help for Problem Behaviours

It usually isn't that the owners are ignoring their dogs' problem behaviours. Often they have tried these or other ways of correcting them to little or no avail. Continuing with the same approaches, however, will only yield the same unsuccessful results. If your dog's behaviour has become a serious problem that you cannot solve alone, you need to seek help.

First, talk to your veterinarian. Sometimes, there can be a medical explanation for your Chihuahua's behaviour. Your vet's advice may be to enrol your dog in a basic obedience-training programme, or consult a professional dog trainer or animal behaviour specialist. Many products are marketed towards desperate dog owners who wish to correct their dogs' problem behaviours. Items that use punishment to control the behaviour—such as shake cans, squirt guns, and anti-bark collars—may at first seem like viable solutions, but with this sensitive breed they can often create more problems than they solve. Establishing better behaviour through fear is less than ideal and will do nothing to form genuinely trustworthy behaviour.

Finding an Animal Behaviour Specialist

The work of an animal behaviourist involves observing, interpreting, and modifying animal behaviour, so he or she can help clients solve their pets' most serious behaviour problems. The biggest difference between behaviourists and other animal trainers or instructors is the severity of the problems they address. Dog trainers and obedience instructors help owners prevent negative behaviours before they become issues. They may also work with owners to correct mild behaviour problems. Behaviourists, on the other hand, deal with more substantial matters.

The advice of a behaviourist may be necessary if your dog suffers from acute anxiety or phobias, aggression, or other behavioural disorders.

Behaviourists do not need any form of licensing to do their

work, so careful selection is a must. Although a certification process does exist, there are currently only a limited number of certified behaviourists. You can find a directory of these individuals at www.apbc.org.uk. Although what is most important is that you are comfortable with the individual you choose, you should also seek a person with a certain level of education and experience dealing with small dogs. A degree in some form of psychology or zoology is a definite advantage. The person should also possess dog training knowledge and experience. References from former clients are good, but recommendations from vets are even better.

Seek the help of a professional trainer or behaviourist if your dog exhibits serious or potentially dangerous problem behaviours.

ADVANCED TRAINING AND ACTIVITIES
With Your Chihuahua

Certainly the Chihuahua is not the first dog many people would consider if seeking an athletic breed to involve in physical activities, such as agility and tracking. This underestimated dog will often surprise them, though, if given the chance. Chihuahuas are strong, quick, and adept animals. They are also highly intelligent. This combination makes them very real contenders in advanced training. In one sense they even have an advantage. Since the breed is often overlooked by so many drawn to activities like agility and obedience, there is a wealth of unchartered territory just waiting to be claimed by this versatile toy breed in the expansive realm of advanced training.

Just like their human owners, dogs crave both mental and physical stimulation. Long periods of rain or other inclement weather can keep a dog from getting his much-needed daily dose of exercise, and it can also leave him feeling bored and unconnected. Unlike us, our dogs cannot simply head to the gym to squeeze in a cardio routine. Instead, many times they go without their fix of fun and exercise. This can lead to a number of problem behaviours. Organised activities can be a productive solution to this problem and a constructive way to spend time with your Chihuahua.

CANINE GOOD CITIZEN SCHEME

Earning a Good Citizen Dog Scheme title is a way to offer proof of your Chihuahua's good behaviour. The Good Citizen Dog Scheme is a training programme that was designed by the Kennel Club. It was launched in 1992, and since then in excess of 52,000 dogs in the United Kingdom have passed the test.

The Good Citizen Dog Scheme is aimed at all dogs, pedigrees and non-pedigrees, regardless of whether they are registered with the Kennel Club. There is no age limit for dogs taking part.

The American Kennel Club's Good Citizen Programme

The AKC Canine Good Citizen (CGC) Programme is a certification series begun in 1989. Stressing responsible pet ownership, the programme rewards dogs that display good manners both at home and in the community.

A 10-step test is administered before certificates are awarded.

All owners must sign a Responsible Dog Owners Pledge before taking the test.

The test focuses on the dog's mastery of basic obedience and his ability to interact peaceably with both human and canine strangers.

There are three levels of award to aim for. These are bronze, silver and gold, with each level becoming increasingly more difficult. Although the exercises differ between levels, they include:

•Accepting a friendly stranger: The friendly stranger will approach and greet the dog's handler. The dog must remain quiet.

• Sitting politely for petting: This will occur while a friendly stranger pets the dog's head and body.

• Appearance and grooming: This involves two steps. First, the evaluator checks that the dog is clean, groomed, and in good condition. Then, the dog must permit a stranger to comb or brush him and check his ears and front feet.

• Out for a walk: This requires the dog to walk quietly on a loose lead, making several turns and stops.

• Walking through a crowd: This step requires the dog and handler to walk politely around and among at least three people.

•Sit and down on command and staying in place: The dog is required to sit, lie down, and stay on command.

•Coming when called: This step requires the dog to stay on command and then come when called from a set distance.

• Reaction to another dog: The dog should react with only casual interest when meeting another dog and handler.

•Reaction to distraction: The dog should react calmly to two common distractions (for instance, a chair falling over, a jogger running by, a wheelchair passing by, or a dropped crutch or stick).

•supervised separation: The dog should remain calm when left with the evaluator while his handler goes out of sight for three minutes.

OBEDIENCE

The difference between practicing obedience skills with your Chihuahua at home or as part of a class and competing in formal obedience trials may be subtle to some owners, while quite significant to others. Your perspective may largely depend on both your own personality and the general temperament of your dog. A Chihuahua should be extremely friendly if involved with formal obedience. Many dogs can be socialised, of course, but a natural affinity for people is a major advantage.

Larger Chihuahuas also seem to fare better in obedience than smaller ones, since jumping many inches will be necessary. Your dog should have a sound structure with no major faults of the front or rear assembly. This will significantly lessen the likelihood of injury.

Once you decide to begin obedience training with your dog, one of your most important decisions will be your selection of a trainer. Ideally, you want someone whom both you and your dog like. Ask as many questions as possible before committing to a training schedule. Listen to your instincts, and pay attention to your dog's reactions to this person, as well. Obedience training should be fun—not stressful for either you or your Chihuahua.

Since larger dogs who are also still in the process of training can inadvertently hurt your toy dog, it is best to seek a class specifically designed for smaller breeds. This will help your Chihuahua gain the confidence necessary to participate in this activity. If you constantly feel you need to pick your dog up or protect him in another similar way, your dog will not likely develop the confidence necessary for this activity. Additionally, many of the methods that work best for training large dogs are simply not transferable to toy breeds. Your dog needs a trainer familiar with an animal of his size and stature.

Obedience training should be fun—not stressful for either you or your Chihuahua.

As a Chihuahua owner, you may have to work a little harder with your dog than other handlers to make strides in the ring. No concessions are made for the Chihuahua's smaller size, so your dog must be comfortable in the expansive environment that may at first seem extremely large and intimidating. It may well be worth the extra effort, though. Not only is obedience fun and rewarding on its own, but many dog owners also consider obedience the foundation upon which all other canine activities are based.

THERAPY WORK

Therapy is an important area in which Chihuahuas can help enhance the human/canine bond by providing unconditional love, companionship, and emotional suipport to residents and patients in nursing homes, hospitals, and children's homes.

Owners volunteering with their Chihuahuas make regularly

Equipment

One challenge you may face is finding the right-sized equipment for your Chihuahua. Collars and leads should both fit properly. Also, if using food rewards, remember that these also must be smaller than standard-sized training treats. A good trainer should be able to help point you towards all the appropriate accoutrement.

scheduled visits and birghten the lives of residents by providing stimulation, and companionship.

Only Chihuahuas who are well-mannered and have a sound temperament should undertake this work. While it is personally satisfying to see how dogs can brighten the lives of residents, 90 percent of the work is done by the dogs, and they must have the physical and mental fortitude to cope with strange noises and smells, distractions, and occasionally erratic behaviour.

Some therapy dogs work extremely well with children; others work best with senior citizens. Many Chihuahuas are better suited for the latter. Sadly, many nursing home residents have begun to lose touch with their family members and other human caregivers. Perhaps as a result of their curious healing touch, dogs often manage to break through the barriers of time and connect with these souls in a way no others can. In the UK, the governing body for therapy dogs is Pets as Therapy (PAT). For detailed information on registering your Chihuahua as a PAT dog, visit their website (www.petsastherapy.org).

SPORTING EVENTS
Agility

Agility is one of the fastest growing sports for dogs in the UK and one of the most exciting, fast-paced canine sports for spectators. It is an extension of obedience but without all the formality and precision. Agility courses are more reminiscent of equestrian courses that include assorted jumps and hurdles. In agility, dogs demonstrate their agile nature and versatility by manoeuvring through a timed obstacle course of jumps, tunnels, A-frames, weave poles, see-saws, ramps, and a pause box. Unlike the higher levels of obedience, agility handlers are permitted to talk to their dogs, and even to give multiple comands.

There are a number of different levels of agility competition. Dogs progress from starters level, to novice, intermediate and advanced level. At each level, the courses are tougher, with increasingly difficult handling points.

The challenge of agility is to be able to control your dog in a wide open area, and direct him to go where you want. It looks easy enough, but courses are set with twists, turns and sometimes with deliberate traps, which can tempt your dog to take the wrong course. If a dog takes the wrong course he is eliminated. He loses points for refusals, knocked poles, and missed contact points. The winner is the dog who completes a clear round in the fastest time.

Agility events in the UK are run under Kennel Club rules, and dogs are not allowed to compete until they are 18 months of age. This is a safeguard to protect bones and joints, which are vulnerable while a dog is still growing.

Even if you do not want to reach competitive level, you and your Chihuahua can still enjoy agility as a fun, non-competitive pastime. Most training organisations have classes for beginners. You will need good basic obedience such as a solid "down", "wait" and "come" before you are ready to even start thinking about taking up agility at a fun level.

The number one consideration in an agility class is safety. This is one of the few sports that can result in serious injuries. Falling off an A-frame or dog walk can break bones. Neglecting to warm up before jumping can cause serious muscle injuries. Out-of-control dogs who are off-lead can also hurt other dogs. Before you sign up for a class, visit a class in action. Does the trainer emphasise safety? Are the larger dogs under control? If the answers are "yes" sign up! You and your Chihuahua will have a great time together.

If you want to start in agility with your dog your first port of call should be a local agility club, ring the secretary or instructor there and discuss your dog, the level of training you currently have

Many Chihuahuas are suited as therapy dogs for senior citizens.

and any health or fitness problems that your dog may suffer–agility is a physically demanding sport even at a fun level. Ask if you can come to watch the training and talk to people with experience, you may be invited to take your dog along so that he can be assessed for fitness and obedience. To find a local agility club in your area, contact the Kennel Club (www.thekennelclub.org.uk) or your national breed club. If you know other dog owners who take part in agility, word of mouth recommendation is also a great place to start, although you should always

check the trainer or club's credentials for yourself.

The biggest drawback to agility is the difficulty many owners face making room to practice the manoeuvres with their dogs. The necessary equipment takes up a great deal of space and is extremely cumbersome to repeatedly assemble and unassemble. This equipment, which consists of numerous pieces, can also be rather expensive.

Many people wonder if the Chihuahua's size is a hindrance when competing in this sport. Surprisingly, Chihuahuas are impressively adept and confident in the agility ring, perhaps in part due to the enthusiastic response they always seem to elicit from the audience. There is, after all, something especially inspiring about seeing this tiny canine prove that he can indeed do virtually anything the bigger dogs can do.

If you are interested in involving your Chihuahua in agility, but worry about the possibility of injury, schedule a physical examination with your dog's veterinarian and ask about the specific risks involved (based on your dog's health and current fitness level). If your dog is not accustomed to intense physical activity, your vet may suggest easing into a more concentrated routine. Although each dog is different, the general threat of injury to a Chihuahua is no greater than that of any other breed.

Agility obstacles include colourful jumps, walks, seesaws, A-frames, and tunnels.

Can My Dog Compete in More Than One Advanced Activity?

The short answer is yes. There are no rules stating that a show dog cannot compete in obedience, or that an obedience competitor cannot participate in agility. Many dogs participate in two or more advanced training activities without a problem. Some dogs, along with their owners, thrive on involvement in a variety of challenging activities.

Others insist that many times one activity can interfere with or limit a dog's success in another. A dog who has gone through a painstaking process to achieve titles in obedience, for instance, may have a hard time adapting to the innate freedoms of agility. Another dog with a similar past could take to agility quite well, but regress in his mastery of obedience, while yet another may succeed in both activities equally well.

You know your dog best. If you think you both might enjoy a new activity, try it. You are always free to take a break from one activity and then come back to it if a new one ends up not being the one for you and your Chihuahua. The most important thing is that both you and your dog are having fun.

Do be careful, though, not to over-schedule either yourself or your dog. These activities, while serious in nature, are meant to be enjoyable. If they start feeling like obligations, or if your dog seems to be losing his fondness for them, it may be time to think about reducing the number of events you attend regularly.

Working Trials

Chihuahuas do very well at working trials, as the breed is able to use its natural abilities to perfom tasks that will satisfy its mental and physical needs. Working trials is a competitive discipline in which dogs are assessed on a variety of working skills and abilities. Dogs must progress through levels of increasing difficulty knows as "stakes". The stakes are; Companion Dog (CD), Utility Dog (UD), Working Dog (WD), Tracking Dog (TD), and Patrol Dog (PD).

Each stake is comprised of three sections: nosework, agility and control. Nosework tests the dog's ability to follow a scent trail.

Agility as the name suggests, assesses a dog's physical agility. Canine competitors have to successfully negotiate a number of obstacles, including jumps.

The control section involves some traditional obedience-style exercises, including heelwork, a sendaway and retrieve.

In the Patrol Dog stake, there is an extra section called manwork, in which the dog must successfully apprehend and control a 'criminal'.

Points are awarded for each exercise, and if the dog is awarded enough points, he achieves the title for that stake and is eligible for entry into the next level. The dog must obtain a minimum of 70 percent of the marks available in each section, as well as 80 percent or more of the total marks overall, to be awarded the Excellent

Kennel Club Sporting Events

The Kennel Club in the United Kingdom sponsors a variety of events for dogs and their owners to enjoy together. For complete listings, rules, and descriptions, please refer to the Kennel Club's website at www.thekennelclub.org.uk.

Agility

Introduced in 1978 at Crufts, agility is a fun, fast-paced, and interactive sport. The event mainly consists of multiple obstacles on a timed course that a dog must handle. Different classes have varying levels of difficulty.

Flyball

Flyball is an exciting sport introduced at Crufts in 1990. Competition involves a relay race in which several teams compete against each other and the clock. Equipment includes hurdles, a flyball box, backstop board, and balls.

Obedience

Obedience competitions test owner and dog's ability to work together as a team. There are three types of obedience tests, which include the Limited Obedience Show, Open Obedience Show, and Championship Obedience Show. Competition becomes successively more difficult with each type of show.

Field Trials

Field trials are designed to test a gundog's ability to work in his natural environment and under competitive conditions. These trials are very similar to a day of hunting in the field, and a variety of game is used.

Gundog Working Tests (GWTs)

Gundog Working Tests are designed to test a dog's natural working ability while promoting sound gundog work. There are three different types of Gundog Working Tests, and each is designed for different breeds of dog.

Working Trials

The first working trial took place in 1924 and was held by the Associated Sheep, Police, and Army Dog Society. Working trials test a dog's working ability and include five levels of competition known as stakes. Each stake is made up of exercises in control, agility, and nosework.

qualification in each stake e.g. C.Dex, UDex etc. Except for the CD the dog must first gain a Certificate of Merit at an Open Trial to enable him to compete in the relevant Championship Stake.

Know Your Dog's Physical Limits

Although Chihuahuas can generally do anything a larger breed can, there are some dogs that should not be involved in certain physical activities. Puppies less than eight months old should avoid rigorous jumping, as the landing process can easily injure their immature legs. Overweight dogs can also easily injure their joints and ligaments, even when adjustments to the courses are made to compensate for their added size and related decreased abilities.

If you wish to involve your Chihuahua in any intense physical activity, it is best to first consult your veterinarian, just as you would your own physician before starting a new exercise regimen for yourself. Your vet is the best person to advise you on how to ease your very young or even older dog into these fun and worthwhile hobbies. An advanced training activity can be a great way to spend time with your Chihuahua, while doing something good for both of you. Taking the proper precautions will ensure that your dog gets the very most out of the pastime.

Although your Chihuahua will likely enjoy taking short walks with you, it is best to leave your dog home if you plan to jog or even walk at a brisk pace. Even the healthiest Chihuahua will quickly become exhausted after jogging at a human's pace for just a short period of time. This overexertion can lead to low blood sugar, seizures, or even a heart attack. Just like too much food, excessive exercise is not good for your Chihuahua's health. If you are a runner, consider going jogging alone (or with a friend) and then including your dog in a more relaxed cool-down period at the end of your workout. This will meet both your needs without overwhelming your dog.

GAMES

Some owners prefer to train and exercise their dogs in less structured settings, perhaps at home in their gardens. This more relaxed approach can serve as a basis for more conventional training down the road, or be used for nothing more than pure fun for you and your dog. By observing your Chihuahua during this kind of play, you can also gain much insight into his learning style and potential for

Sports and Safety

You would never begin working out without taking the time to warm up, and neither should your Chihuahua! Just like a human being, a dog needs to raise his core body temperature, heart rate, and respiration rate before participating in any kind of sport or intense exercise to help prevent injuries. Blood pressure increases more quickly without a warm-up period, so just taking this easy step reduces the workload on your dog's heart. Warming up also delivers much-needed oxygen to the muscles, lowering the chance of muscle strain.

You can provide your dog with a sufficient warm-up period by simply setting aside a few extra minutes before any activity for a brief walk or toned-down version of the sport (i.e., the same activity, but at a lower intensity level). Warming up can also improve skill and coordination, two vital components to success in most advanced training competitions.

When your dog is finished competing, don't forget to finish with a proper cooldown! This return to low-intensity activity will help your dog's blood continue to circulate from the muscles and also help dissipate heat. You can use the same routine and activity level for your Chihuahua's cooldown as you did for his warmup.

Keep exercise appropriate for your tiny friend—even the healthiest of Chihuahuas couldn't keep up with jogging at a human's pace.

different activities. A dog that likes to run and jump may be well suited for agility, whereas a dog that seems to look to you for direction during play may be an excellent candidate for obedience.

The best thing about all these activities is that you are not required to continue up a ladder of success. A friend of mine has a very intelligent dog that especially enjoys the tunnels in agility, but shows no interest in any of the other obstacles. Agility competitions are not for this animal, but she still has a load of fun streaming through the vivid nylon passageways in her own garden nonetheless. Listening to the cues your dog gives you about what he most likes and dislikes is one of the best things you can do to meet your dog's needs and create rewarding pastimes for you both.

Playing Ball

Many dogs enjoy playing ball, and the Chihuahua is no exception, although catching the ball in his delicate mouth can be a difficult task for this tiny canine. The best way to play ball with your Chihuahua is by bouncing the ball gently away from the dog, allowing him to run after it, or by rolling the ball slowly towards your dog.

Fetch

Fetch is a game that can be played with any toy your Chihuahua fancies. Keep in mind, however, that your dog might not be especially keen on giving up a particularly treasured item once he has taken possession of it. This can be part of the fun for your dog, but discontinue play if your dog's possessiveness escalates to aggressive behaviour.

Follow the Leader

Many Chihuahuas are naturals at follow the leader. Using various kinds of impromptu obstacles, this game can easily be played in a garden, or inside the home using furniture, hallways, and other items within your home as your props. Placing a reward, such as a favourite toy or other treat, at the end of the course can be a fun addition.

Hide and Seek

Hide and seek is a great way to practice the sit, stay, and come commands with your Chihuahua. After giving the first two commands, find a place to hide and then call your dog. Remember to reward him for finding you. You can also hide a treat for your dog to find. As your Chihuahua becomes more and more adept at locating the treat, try hiding additional treats—laying the groundwork for a treasure hunt.

Toys

Don't forget toys! Toys can be a great motivator to get your dog moving. Saving one or two special items for more active playtimes can help ensure that your dog will be willing to participate in a good old-fashioned game of fetch when the time comes. Toys are also a great nonedible reward to use at the end of an informal training session.

Fetch can be played with any toy your Chihuahua fancies.

Believe it or not, some dogs can be taught to pick up and put away their own toys. A variation of playing fetch, this game of sorts can be a fun and useful way to cap off each play session. Like many other games, it can also be a great foundation for further training activities.

Seize the opportunity for play whenever your schedule allows. You don't need big chunks of time! Your Chihuahua will actually get more out of several shorter periods of play throughout the day than he will from one longer, exhausting session.

As with more organised activities, it is best to end games on a positive note. If you quit playing while your Chihuahua is still having fun, the dog will be more interested in joining in the fun next time. This will help maintain your dog's attention if you do wish to incorporate training into future playtimes.

SHOWING YOUR CHIHUAHUA
The Characteristics of a Show Dog

Good Chihuahua breeders look for two main things in their puppies: Good temperaments and the physical qualities that most closely match the breed standard. Unquestionably the more important of the two, congenial personalities make dogs suitable pets—more open to learning and training, less prone to aggression and problem behaviours, and easier to match to loving prospective owners. Dogs with good temperaments are also essential to breeders for producing future litters of similarly good-natured puppies. Dogs who are both amiable and attractive are often retained for this purpose. When a Chihuahua comes along who possesses virtually all of the breed's most coveted traits, both aesthetically and temperamentally, this dog will also best represent the breed in the show ring.

Dog shows, also called conformation events, evaluate just how closely the entrants match their breed's standard, an indication of an animal's ability to produce quality puppies. Showing is in fact a means of evaluating breeding stock; therefore, spayed and neutered dogs may not participate. A member of the toy group, the Chihuahua is no stranger to the ring.

How Dog Shows Work

Before a Chihuahua, or any breed, can be entered into a conformation show, he must meet certain criteria. A complete list of rules and regulations governing eligibility may be obtained from the KC, but basic guidelines require that your dog be a purebred registered Chihuahua.

Dog shows can seem pretty complicated when you first attend one and try to work out what is going on, even as a spectator. But this is a highly organised sport. Dogs are trying to earn that coveted title of Champion and to do this, a dog must earn three Challenge Certificates under three different judges. Challenge Certificates are on offer only at Championship shows, and in these competitions the best male and female will be awarded a CC.

In a dog show, dogs are individually exhibited by their handlers. This can be the pet owner, the breeder, or a professional handler. In the US, professional handlers are used in high-profile dog shows, but in the UK most Chihuahuas are handled by their owners. Handlers bring the dogs out into the ring and the judge examines each one, and also watches all the dogs move around the ring. Typically, the judge eliminates all but a handful at first, then even more carefully studies the finalists.

At the first level, dogs are divided into classes, and in each class, males and females are judged separately. Prizes will be awarded to dogs in the highest places. When the judge has finished judging all the classes, it is time to find the overall winners.

The judge must look at his class winners and select the best male and the best female. This is no easy task, as he will be evaluating dogs of different ages, from puppies of a mere six months of age, right up to advanced, experienced show dogs. A number of dogs may already be Champions, so it is a very tough challenge for young, upcoming

Make sure you give your Chihuahua appropriate chew toys to help maintain a healthy mouth and relieve boredom.

What to Wear When Showing Your Chihuahua

It is understandable to want to look your best when showing your dog. Judges and spectators usually dress up for shows, as well, so it would seem logical that matching their standards of attire would be the best way to show respect for the event. While this is certainly true, it is equally important for handlers to dress appropriately for the ring. The right clothes help you show your dog to his best advantage.

Select clothing that reflects both class and comfort. You will need clothes that allow you to bend or kneel as necessary, and this can be difficult in a restrictive suit or ladylike skirt. There is certainly nothing wrong with wearing a suit, as long as it allows you to move freely about the ring. Trousers and split skirts are freeing alternatives to dresses and more traditional skirts for female handlers. A versatile choice for male handlers is a pair of trousers paired with a well-tailored blazer.

Avoid bold prints or clothing that clashes with your dog's features. Colours and fabrics should not detract from your dog's appearance, but contrast is often advantageous. Remember, your Chihuahua should be the one drawing everyone's attention.

dogs to come forward.

The judge will make his choice and will select his winning male and female. If Challenge Certificates are on offer, both dogs will be awarded a CC. However, there is one final honour the breed judge can award—and that is Best of Breed. The judge will make a thorough evaluation of each dog, and will then declare a Best of Breed.

In a breed show, the Best of Breed winner is equivalent to winning Best in Show. But in an all-breed show the Best of Breed (BOB) still has a way to go. The next step is to compete in the Group ring.

Subsequently, the winners from all of the Groups go forward to the Best in Show ring. In a large dog show it is a great accomplishment to win Best in Show.

Breeders consider the number of BIS titles won in a dog's career a serious indicator of quality for breeding stock, and indeed it is. Because remember, that is the original point of this whole complicated event. A Chihuahua with multiple BIS parents is probably going to be an excellent example of a Chihuahua, as it is meant to be.

Getting Started

If you are interested in participating in conformation events, begin by first attending shows as a spectator. If the grooming area is open to the public, introduce yourself to the other Chihuahua owners there, and ask if they would mind telling you about their experiences with showing. Although this is a competitive environment, there are many extremely kind and outgoing people involved in the activity who are willing to help newcomers and who also enjoy sharing their enthusiasm for the breed with other kindred spirits.

In addition to exhibitors, vendors and information stands can also be valuable resources. If you are still considering purchasing your first Chihuahua, these are all wonderful starting points. Most of the breeders at these events are among the very best and can help point you towards a show-quality dog if this is what you are seeking.

If you have already purchased your dog, consider joining your local Chihuahua club. You will likely find that the organisation offers classes for conformation training. Entering this sport and absorbing all the necessary information can be overwhelming. By taking it slow and learning as much as you can, you will help ensure a positive experience for both you and your dog.

Like other advanced training activities, showing requires great discipline on behalf of both dog and owner, but many people involved find it to be a labour of love. Showing Chihuahuas can serve as a gateway to endless learning about this breed, wonderful friends who share your affinity for it, and an opportunity to strengthen your bond with your special pet.

Crufts

Billed as the "Greatest Dog Show in the World", the Crufts Dog Show is officially recognised by the Guinness Book of Records as the largest one too, with more than 24,000 dogs entered. The four-day event covers 20 acres with nearly 400 retail stands and attracts more than 120,000 visitors.

Handlers

If you wish to become more than casually involved in showing, frequent travelling is a must. Losing can also be traumatic for some participants, particularly beginners, and the criticism of the show ring can be overwhelming for many owners. For these and many other reasons, some owners decide to hire professional handlers to show their dogs for them. Saving an owner the time and hassle of constant travel and direct show participation, a handler is a practical alternative for people who wish to show their dogs but do not wish to do so themselves.

If you decide to hire a handler, be sure to do your research thoroughly before entrusting the individual with your precious Chihuahua. You want someone who has experience showing toy breeds and, more importantly, someone who will treat your dog as you would in any situation that might arise. A resume filled with championship titles only matters if your dog will be treated with love and respect.

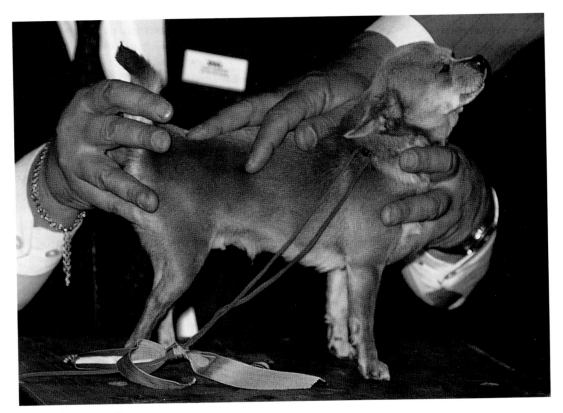

Show dogs must tolerate travel, strangers, meticulous grooming, and the noise of crowds.

Do What's Best for Your Chihuahua

You may find that your dog simply does not have what it takes to compete in this activity. Show dogs must tolerate travel, strangers (both human and canine), meticulous grooming, and the noise of crowds all in stride—and meet the aesthetic standards for competition. In most cases, unless you purchased a dog already designated as potential show material, the chances of your Chihuahua excelling in the conformation ring are relatively slim.

If your dog is a poor fit for conformation, consider one of the other advanced training activities that may be a better fit for the two of you. The perfect show dog may be out there waiting for someone to buy him, but your Chihuahua is here now and needs your time and attention—and he just may be destined for greatness in another type of event.

Showing in the US

Although the showing process of the Kennel Club is relatively similar to that of the AKC, the road to championship there is

Finding Common Ground— The Two Types of Chihuahua Owners

Chihuahua lovers often decidedly place themselves into one of two categories: Show dog (or performance dog) owners and pet owners. Sadly, many believe these choices are mutually exclusive, but both ways of enjoying your dog are possible. Many show dogs are first and foremost much-loved family members. Many dogs without champions in their pedigree are also quite capable of making strides in activities such as conformation, obedience, and agility.

One choice is no better than the other. Whether your dog has garnered several titles, or your Chihuahua's biggest accomplishment is having you wrapped around his paw, what matters most is that both you and your dog are content. There is a tremendous amount of pride involved in helping your dog achieve notoriety in advanced training, but being a loving and committed dog owner is a highly respectable accomplishment itself.

considerably different. In the UK there is no point system. Instead judges award dogs with Challenge Certificates. It is left up to the judge to decide how many dogs are worthy of this honour, so the overall number of entrants is somewhat irrelevant. Competition can be fierce, though, with shows often extending over several days each.

In order to obtain championship status, a dog must receive three Challenge Certificates from three different judges. One of these certificates must be awarded after the dog is 12 months old.

For many years criticism has been made that Challenge Certificates are given out far too often, and that less than completely deserving dogs have received them. As a means of ensuring proper understanding of the criteria, the Kennel Club General Committee changed the wording of the official regulations for this award, effective January 1, 2005.

Another difference is the focused area of expertise of British judges compared to American judges. In Britain, judges who specialise in one particular breed are far more common. Since they have had such vast experience with the dogs they breed (or have bred in the past), these judges are considered the best authorities on that breed by the KC. An AKC judge is much more likely to judge several different breeds, having accumulated knowledge of them all without necessarily breeding all of them personally.

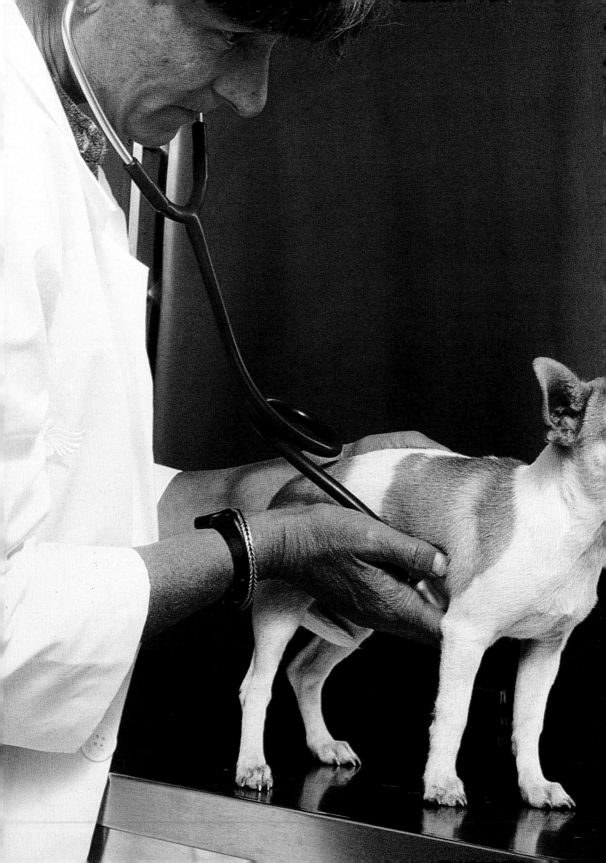

C h a p t e r

8

HEALTH

of Your Chihuahua

C hihuahuas are remarkably hardy little dogs. When cared for properly, this devoted breed has the potential of sharing your life for many years. In return for his love and companionship, your beloved pet deserves the very best of care. There are many ways of pampering your dog—from providing him with numerous toys to spending countless hours with your pup playing with him—but without routine veterinary care, your dog will be placed at risk for a variety of problems. The best way to show your Chihuahua you love him is by nurturing his health.

FINDING THE BEST VETERINARIAN FOR YOUR CHIHUAHUA

Countless decisions come with owning a dog—one of the most important is your choice of a veterinarian. Your Chihuahua's vet is much more than just the person who gives your dog his shots. Ideally, you should choose someone who genuinely cares about animals, possesses specific knowledge about Chihuahuas, and makes both you and your dog feel comfortable during your visits. This might seem like a tall order, but in the event of a medical crisis, you will be very thankful for having been so discriminating in your selection process.

Support staff (receptionists and veterinary technicians) set the tone for your visits. Friendly, well-informed people who make you feel welcome can make a good veterinarian stand out among the rest. Similarly, a rude staff member who isn't good with animals or makes a pet owner feel like an inconvenience can make even the best doctor seem unworthy of your time.

Other important factors might include location and cost of services. Knowing your dog is in the best hands possible is usually well worth driving a few extra miles or paying a bit more than first expected, but you must also be realistic. If your Chihuahua doesn't tolerate travelling well, a significantly longer trip may cause unnecessary stress for the animal. Although you shouldn't base your choice on the surgery's prices alone, money must also be considered. If you always struggle to pay your dog's bill, you may be more likely to

Emergencies! When You Need to Act Fast

The following situations are considered medical emergencies. If your dog experiences any of these problems, get him to the nearest veterinary surgery as soon as possible.

- Animal bites or insect stings
- Breathing difficulties
- Broken bones
- Choking
- Frequent vomiting
- Paralysis
- Poisoning
- Scalds or burns
- Seizures
- Severe diarrhoea
- Severe trauma (from a fall or traffic accident, for example)
- Temperature-related injuries (such as heatstroke, frostbite, or hypothermia)
- Wounds with excessive bleeding

postpone an important visit, one of the biggest mistakes a dog owner can make.

The worst time to begin looking for a veterinarian is when your Chihuahua needs medical care right away. Start your search the moment you decide to add a Chihuahua to your household. If your breeder's vet isn't located too far from your home, this could be an excellent starting point. Other useful resources for referrals are local breed clubs, animal shelters, and sometimes even friends and family members. Ask other dog owners you trust who their vets are, and more importantly, if they would recommend them and why. Call to arrange a tour of the veterinary facility, so you can meet the staff and get a feel for the environment. A veterinary surgery doesn't have to be fancy or modern looking, but it should be clean and well organised. Unwillingness to allow a tour is a red flag.

Questions to Ask When Looking for a Veterinarian

Ask numerous questions, and write them down in advance. Are emergencies handled on the premises or referred to an emergency clinic? How many veterinarians are on staff? Will the same vet see your dog for every visit? Your preferences in these areas are generally matters of personal choice.

Other questions demand more specific responses. Will you be referred to a specialist if your Chihuahua's needs exceed the vet's expertise? Beware of doctors who refuse to acknowledge their limitations. Is there a separate area for treating infectious animals? Does the facility offer 24-hour care for hospitalised pets? It is particularly important that patients are monitored after certain surgical procedures where bleeding is a concern.

The staff, including the veterinarian, should answer your questions directly and in language you can understand. Communication between you and your dog's vet is essential. You and your vet should be partners in your dog's care, and you should be consulted regarding all decisions that are part of the process.

Your Responsibilities

Just as your veterinarian has a duty to care for your Chihuahua, as his owner you also have responsibilities to both your dog and the vet. It is your job to make healthy choices for your dog by offering him a nutritious diet, providing ample exercise, and keeping up with essential grooming, such as regular teeth brushing.

Giving your dog thorough home care can help the vet give your dog the best possible veterinary care.

As you get to know your new Chihuahua, take note of what is normal for your dog, and bring him in for an examination at the first sign of illness. Equally important as sick visits are routine checkups, for these can identify small problems before they become more serious. Never skip a well visit.

You also owe it to your veterinarian to be a conscientious client. This means making appointments, being punctual, and bringing along any necessary stool or urine samples requested by the vet. Depending on your doctor's protocol, it may also be wise to call first even in an emergency. The last thing you want to hear as you walk through the door to your veterinary surgery with your Chihuahua in an emergency is that the veterinarian has left for the day.

If you live a fair distance from the vet you think is best, geography doesn't have to rule out this caregiver. As long as it isn't too far for normal visits, you can use this vet as your dog's primary vet, and establish a working relationship with another veterinarian, closer to home, for more time–sensitive needs.

Pet Insurance

The cost of health care can be a demanding part of dog ownership. Advancing medical technologies have lifted veterinary medicine to a level more comparable to human care than it has ever been. Especially if you have more than one pet, the price of even routine care can be draining. Chronic conditions requiring frequent veterinary visits and costly medications can be particularly taxing both emotionally and financially. Because of this, many Chihuahua owners decide to protect their pets with medical insurance.

Similar to human health insurance carriers, several national companies offer pet policies that reimburse owners for such expenses as emergency care, prescriptions, and in some cases even routine physicals and preventive medications (such as flea control). Unlike human health plans, though, many of these policies do not require that you use a specific doctor. No owner should ever have to base a life-saving decision for their pet on their finances, so ask your veterinarian about this option if you think it might be helpful to you. If you wait until your dog is sick or injured, the problem may be labelled a pre-existing condition, resulting in higher premiums and possibly even denial of coverage for the problem.

Emergency Veterinary Clinics

Whether your primary veterinarian is 5 minutes or 15 miles (24.1 km) away, you should familiarise yourself with the emergency veterinary clinics in your area. Emergency clinics usually open when other surgeries are closing down for the day and stay open until their more conventional counterparts re-open the next morning. Some are open 24 hours a day. You will pay more for the care at emergency clinics, but they are usually the only vets available at odd hours. Check to see if your primary veterinarian has an out of hours service and make a record of the number.

If you are unsure of whether your dog needs emergency treatment, call your nearest emergency veterinary surgery. A staff member should be able to tell you if your dog's condition warrants immediate examination, or if you can wait for an appointment with your regular veterinarian. If the emergency vet does see your dog, you will be instructed to follow up with your primary veterinarian at an appropriate time.

YOUR CHIHUAHUA'S FIRST CHECKUP

You should make your Chihuahua's first veterinary appointment as soon as possible—at the very latest within a week of the dog's homecoming. Bring your dog's vaccination schedule and any other health-related paperwork with you. Most likely you will be asked to also bring along a stool sample; feeding your Chihuahua about an hour before leaving the house should yield a proper specimen. (A plastic sandwich bag works well for collection.)

Once at the veterinarian's office, a technician will weigh your dog and take his temperature. You will be asked a series of questions about your dog's medical history, and about how he has behaved since arriving in his new home. The vet will examine your dog from head to tail, including his eyes, ears, and teeth, heart and lungs, and joints and kneecaps. Depending on your Chihuahua's

The vet will examine your Chihuahua from head to tail.

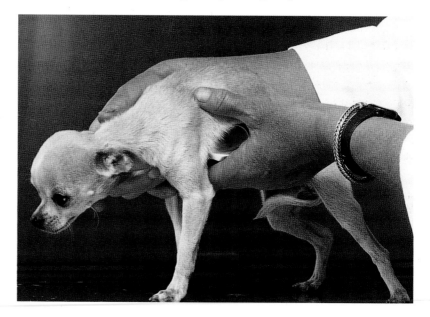

age, it may also be time for certain vaccinations.

Your vet will ask if you would like advice about diet, housetraining, and general dog care. This is the time to ask any questions you may have for your vet regarding your dog's health and behaviour. New dog owners are often sent home with information packs, containing pamphlets about veterinary health care and samples of pet care products. At home, read the handouts thoroughly, and make a point to ask any questions you might still have at your Chihuahua's next appointment. If your question is a pressing one, call the office and ask a staff member before then; a good veterinary surgery should always be willing to answer your questions.

Your breeder will have already begun your Chihuahua's vaccination process by the time you take him home. Other vaccinations, such as distemper and

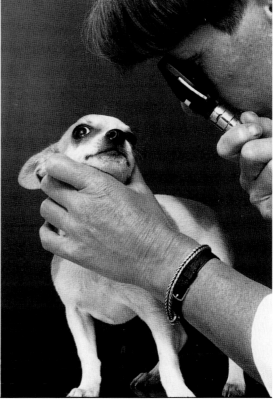

Your Chihuahua's eyes will be checked for any signs of infection.

parvovirus, will require booster shots (repeated doses that ensure effectiveness), so you will be seeing your dog's vet frequently during the first few weeks. Once your dog has received all his vaccinations, it will then be time to consider scheduling an appointment for spaying or neutering. After that, your dog should only need to be seen for annual checkups, or in the event of any illness or injury.

What Every Owner Needs to Know About Vaccinations

The most routine procedure performed by veterinarians, vaccinations are a dog's best defence against many deadly diseases. Still, vaccinations are a controversial topic within the dog community—even veterinarians themselves occasionally disagree about which vaccines are safe and how often they should be administered. The dangers of over-vaccinating dogs are subjects of constant research, and the findings can sometimes be rather

Talk to your veterinarian about a vaccination schedule for your Chihuahua.

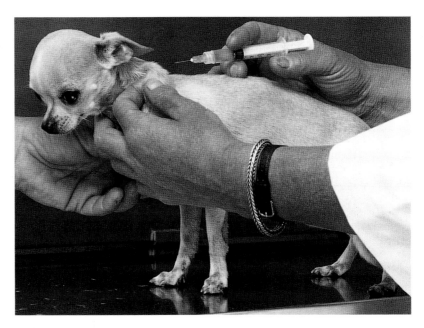

confusing. Just as parents are educating themselves more about the vaccines offered to their infants and toddlers, pet owners are also becoming better informed about the benefits and liabilities of conventional vaccination schedules.

A vaccination essentially stimulates your dog's immune system to protect itself from disease. When a vaccine is injected into your Chihuahua's body, it is instantly recognised as a foreign agent. Antibodies are then produced to destroy it, setting an important precedent. The next time your dog's body is confronted with the same intruder, it will recognise the agent and respond even more quickly than the first time. Mimicking the body's own talent for creating immunity, vaccinations generally prevent a dog from falling victim to particular illnesses.

Some immunologists and veterinarians point out that problems can appear, though, when an animal is given too many different vaccines together or unnecessary repeated doses annually. Many experts insist that not only does immunity resulting from vaccinations last significantly longer than once believed, but also that continual boosters can actually weaken a dog's immune system, making the animal more vulnerable to such serious problems as acute allergies, epilepsy, and certain autoimmune diseases. One option is asking your veterinarian to only administer one vaccine at a time over several days, but availability of noncombination vaccinations might be a challenge.

Although both sides of the debate present convincing evidence supporting their theories on vaccinations, presently this issue is mostly a judgement call for owners. Skipping the vaccination process altogether, however, is not the answer. Dogs need vaccinations for such deadly diseases as distemper and parvovirus.

Other vaccines and their frequency are a matter of education, circumstance, and preference. You should discuss these vaccines with your veterinarian and select a schedule of which you both approve.

Signs Your Chihuahua Needs Veterinary Care

If you notice any of the following signs, schedule an appointment with your Chihuahua's veterinarian:

- Shortness of breath or coughing, prolonged or heavy panting
- Weight loss or gain
- Decreased appetite
- Increased thirst and urination
- Uncharacteristic housetraining accidents, diarrhoea, or blood in stools
- Recurrent vomiting
- Unexplained trembling
- Change in sleeping habits
- Weakness or fatigue
- Lameness or discomfort when moving
- Bad breath
- Dullness of coat, dry flaky skin, or hair loss
- Any unchecked lumps or bumps
- Any unexplained changes in behaviour

ANNUAL CHECKUPS

Never underestimate the importance of your Chihuahua's annual checkup. Dogs are amazingly resilient creatures and do not always show immediate signs when something is wrong. Many serious health problems can be identified and corrected during routine exams by your dog's veterinarian, but you must make sure to provide the opportunity.

Just as your own doctor gives you a complete physical once a year, your dog's vet will check your dog from head to tail during his yearly exam. Starting with your dog's nose, eyes, ears, and mouth, the vet will look for any signs of infection. The vet will then move on to your dog's heart and lungs, listening for any congestion or other abnormalities. He or she will also check your dog's skin and coat, evaluating its overall lustre and checking for any significant cuts and scrapes while simultaneously looking for signs of any fleas, ticks, or other parasites. The lymph nodes will be checked for symmetry, size, and tenderness. External genitalia will be examined for any abnormal discharge, colour, or swelling. Your Chihuahua's reflexes will be tested, and his general behaviour will be observed. Finally, your dog's entire body will be carefully examined for any unusual lumps or enlarged internal organs.

A technician will weigh your dog before his exam and ask if you have any specific concerns you would like to discuss with the veterinarian. Oftentimes general care issues can be addressed by the tech, but never hesitate to ask your veterinarian any question you may have about your dog's health. As busy as many vets are, they are all working for a single purpose—their patients' well being.

Remember, your Chihuahua cannot always tell you when something is wrong. An annual checkup is your veterinarian's best tool for evaluating your dog's health, so help can be given when needed. It is also a good idea for your dog to visit the vet under circumstances not relating to illness, as this can ease an anxious dog's fears about the veterinary surgery. You might even want to ask your vet if it is okay for you to bring your Chihuahua by occasionally, so he can enjoy a quick visit, maybe eat a healthy treat, and not have to even step onto the scale. This will help show your dog that the veterinarian and other staff members are his friends and that he should always be happy to see them.

SPAYING AND NEUTERING

Frequently referred to as fixing, sterilisation is one of the most valuable decisions a dog owner can make. With this single choice you are increasing your Chihuahua's potential life span, as well as helping to control the ever-growing pet population. With the number of unwanted animals entering rehoming centres each year growing, this is a problem that demands each and every pet owner's attention.

Spaying, the proper term for sterilising a female dog, involves removing the ovaries and uterus so she may not become pregnant. Sterilisation also eliminates the risk of ovarian and uterine cancers and uterine infections, and it significantly reduces the risk of breast cancer later in the dog's life. A spayed female will not go into heat, the state that immediately precedes ovulation in dogs. A female in heat will attract the attention of any male dogs nearby, and she will also bleed during this time.

Neutering, the equivalent procedure for males, consists of removing the testicles, and simultaneously the dog's ability to impregnate a female. This eliminates the risk of testicular cancer, and it also significantly reduces the risk of prostate cancer. Neutered males tend to exhibit fewer annoying behaviours, such as marking territory, excessive barking and howling, and aggression.

Both male and female dogs should be spayed by the time they are six months old unless they will be shown or bred. Statistically, pets that are sterilised by this age live longer than intact dogs. Show dogs or dogs used for breeding should be sterilised after they are done with these activities. Under normal circumstances neither operation carries significant risk to the dog.

With a Chihuahua's extremely small size, however, there are risks associated with giving birth. Chihuahuas are among the five most common dog breeds requiring emergency C-sections. Unless you have experience with breeding Chihuahuas, and your dog exhibits all the desirable qualities of the breed that should be passed on, it is best to leave breeding to others.

Dispelling the Common Myths About Spaying and Neutering

Some owners assume that the long-lived beliefs about spaying and neutering must be true, but the facts are very different from the wives' tales.

- A female dog does not need to go through her first heat or have a litter of puppies before she is spayed. Dogs who have never experienced a heat cycle or had a litter prior to surgery actually have a decreased risk of developing malignant breast cancer later in life.
- Spayed and neutered dogs aren't more prone to obesity than other canines. The metabolisms of sterilised pets change at the same rate as any other dog.
- It is just as important to neuter a male dog as it is to spay a female. Chihuahuas can breed with any other dog breed; size has no bearing on your male dog's ability of impregnating another canine. For his health, as well as the consideration of any female dogs he may encounter, have him neutered.
- Dogs do not need to wait until they are between six months and a year old for spaying or neutering. Most veterinarians recommend having your dog sterilised shortly after the completion of his or her puppy vaccines, around the age of five months. Talk to your veterinarian about the best age for your Chihuahua's surgery, but if possible your dog should be fixed before he or she is six months old.
- Having a dog sterilised does not detract from his or her personality or gender. Although some research suggests that neutering a male dog can lower aggression levels, there will be very little—if any—difference in your dog's general temperament as a result of surgery. Sterilised animals will remain just as loving as they were before surgery, and the same will hold true of their protective instincts over their homes and families. Dogs do not have an understanding of human-imposed gender stereotypes.

THE MOST COMMON HEALTH ISSUES FOR CHIHUAHUAS

Genetic problems are among the most important reasons to do all your homework before choosing a breeder. While there is hardly a breed that has no common problems that might be passed down from one generation to the next, responsible breeders will conduct genetic testing and pull any questionable dogs out of their breeding programmes. Still, there are many issues that may be caused only in part by genetics. It is a good idea to know which problems you might face with your Chihuahua and how to recognise them.

Cleft Palate

Often occurring along with a cleft lip, a cleft palate is a condition in which the two bony plates at the top of the mouth do not join together; this leaves a cleft (a hole or a slit) in the roof of the mouth between the oral and nasal cavities. Chihuahuas with cleft palates are more vulnerable to nasal infections. A cleft palate is usually noticeable at birth, because an affected pup will have trouble nursing; sometimes the mother's milk will even run from the puppy's nose. If the opening is small at birth, it may close on its own. It can also be corrected surgically. Most cleft palates are genetic.

Good breeders conduct genetic testing to keep their Chihuahua puppies as healthy and free of disease as possible.

Collapsed Trachea

A chronic honking sound is a sign of a collapsed trachea, another common health problem in Chihuahuas. The trachea, commonly called the windpipe, is the tube that descends from the larynx carrying air to the dog's lungs. When this tube weakens and ultimately collapses, the airway becomes irritated and respiration becomes an arduous task. Mild cases of this normally genetic condition may be treated successfully with cough suppressants, as well as reductions in excitement and exertion. (Always check with your doctor before giving your dog any medication, though.) In more severe cases, surgery may be necessary. Signs of this disorder include difficulty breathing, fatigue, and exercise intolerance.

Hydrocephalus

While recent research has shown that Chihuahuas with moleras are not predisposed to hydrocephalus, the condition is generally more common in this and other toy breeds. Placing severe pressure on the brain from surrounding fluid, hydrocephalus is a life-threatening condition that requires immediate veterinary attention. It usually occurs in very young dogs—some just a few months old. It may be genetic, triggered by trauma, or a result of other circumstances, such as a brain tumour. Common symptoms are sudden blindness, seizures, or an altered gait. If you witness any of these symptoms in your dog, bring your Chihuahua to his veterinarian immediately.

Hypoglycaemia

Like other toy breeds, Chihuahuas face an increased risk of hypoglycaemia. The medical term for low blood sugar, hypoglycaemia is basically the opposite of diabetes. Most dogs outgrow the problem naturally before they are even old enough to leave their mothers, but in some cases the condition remains a continued threat to the dogs' health.

Symptoms of hypoglycaemia include poor coordination, weakness, and glassy eyes. Seizures are also commonly seen. If your dog exhibits these signs, the first thing you should do is feed him food with a high sugar content, such as syrup or honey. If the dog is especially weak, you may have to put a small amount on your finger and rub it on your dog's gums. Never try to force any food down your dog's throat, as he could choke. The dog should also be kept warm. If your dog readily accepts the treat and can sit on his own, you may want to offer him a small meal. Next, contact your Chihuahua's veterinarian. Even if the episode passes easily with the help of the sugary treat, it is still vital that your vet knows about the incident. He or she will likely ask you to bring your Chihuahua in for an exam at this time.

Hypoglycaemia is a very serious but manageable disease. If left untreated, a hypoglycaemic dog can experience seizures, lose consciousness, or even die. Once a dog is diagnosed, however, his owner can control the disease by feeding smaller, more frequent meals. It is especially important that a dog with this condition doesn't miss a meal, so make arrangements for someone else to feed your Chihuahua if you are ever unable to make it home in time. If you take your dog on regular walks, it may be a good idea to take along liquid glucose packets. These can be purchased at most pharmacies.

Your veterinarian can help you select a food high in protein, fat, and complex carbohydrates that will help your Chihuahua best utilise its nutrients. You will generally want to avoid feeding simple sugars, but you will need to adjust your dog's diet accordingly when his exercise level is increased, as increased activity may justify an increased sugar content. Talk to your vet about the right plan for your dog.

Because your Chihuahua exists so close to the floor, eye injuries may occur.

Luxating Patella

Chihuahuas are especially susceptible to a condition called a luxating patella, a dislocation of a small, flat bone at the front of the dog's knee. Aggravated by excess weight, this loose kneecap can slip out of place occasionally (or frequently), causing your dog to hold up the leg and hop on the other three. In mild cases the condition may be tolerated with the help of anti-inflammatory medication, but surgery can help in more severe instances. In many cases dogs can also develop arthritis as a result of this condition. To prevent both problems, it is especially important to keep your Chihuahua from jumping off furniture or other high objects.

Retained Baby Teeth

Some Chihuahuas have what are called retained baby teeth, primary teeth that do not seem to want to fall out naturally. Usually, providing chew toys and playing tug-of-war type games with your dog can help. Occasionally, surgical extraction by a veterinarian is necessary.

You can certainly try counting your puppy's teeth to see if permanent teeth are naturally replacing lost baby teeth, but it may be difficult to get your dog to cooperate with this process. Your veterinarian can probably give you an accurate count more easily. A Chihuahua puppy will start out with 28 deciduous teeth and by adulthood have 42 permanent teeth.

Retained teeth will cause malocclusion (a bad bite), since they prevent adult teeth from growing in properly. Your Chihuahua's canines (the large teeth that resemble fangs) should point outwards; teeth bending inwards can pierce the roof of the dog's mouth. Overcrowding can also be very uncomfortable for your dog, making everyday activities like chewing painful tasks.

Read the Label!

Although some veterinarians will suggest temporarily feeding a dog baby food after a tooth extraction or other surgery, examine those jars carefully. Many baby foods contain onion powder, which can be toxic for your Chihuahua.

Snoring

Because of their short muzzles, Chihuahuas snore—often loudly. They can also wheeze frequently for similar reasons. Neither condition is serious or causes any pain to your dog under normal circumstances. Although this breed is predisposed to snoring, being overweight can also cause snoring. Sometimes just reducing your dog's weight can curb the problem. If you detect laboured breathing or notice that your dog's sleep is being interrupted, you may want to mention the issue to your veterinarian, as there could be an underlying health problem.

Vision Problems

Chihuahuas are not normally genetically predisposed to eye disorders, but since this breed exists so close to the floor, they are more prone to eye injuries than many other breeds. Any dog can also suffer from degenerative eye diseases.

Cataracts

Cataracts are among the most common reasons for canine blindness. Literally opaque white spots within the lens of the eye, cataracts aren't painful, but in some instances they can lead to more serious conditions that can cause permanent sight loss. Though sometimes inherited, cataracts can also be caused by metabolic changes, such as diabetes. Signs of cataracts include an apparent film on the dog's eye, but actually the cloudy lens is deep inside the eyeball. By replacing the damaged lens with an acrylic lens, a veterinary ophthalmologist can restore an affected dog's vision with a success rate of 90 to 95 percent.

Cherry Eye

Many dog owners do not realise that most domesticated animals have an extra eyelid called the third eyelid. Positioned just below your Chihuahua's lower lid near the nasal side of the eye, it is usually not noticed without careful inspection. Just behind this third eyelid lies a tear gland responsible for 30 percent of the dog's eye lubrication. When this gland becomes swollen or inflamed, it can protrude from behind the third eyelid, creating an unsightly condition called prolapse of the gland of the nictitans. More commonly referred to as cherry eye, it looks very much like it sounds—a raised red mass in the corner of the eye.

Cherry eye is most common in younger dogs and may affect either one or both eyes. Though not painful to the dog, it can be frightening for an unsuspecting owner. It can, however, become

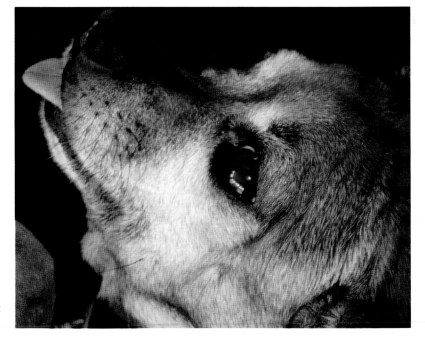

Cataracts are a common cause of canine blindness.

irritated if the gland is exposed for too long and becomes infected. The condition is believed to be genetic, but may also occur in any dog as a result of infection or trauma.

Steroids can be helpful in reducing swelling, but results are usually only temporary, and complications often develop with prolonged use. Surgery is usually a better choice. The procedure consists of repositioning the gland. Surgery also once included the removal of the tear gland of the eyelid, but fewer vets are now taking this additional step. Without this gland, a dog is at greater risk for a condition called keratoconjunctivitis sicca (KCS), or dry eye. KCS is a vision-threatening disease that can result in redness, mucus discharge, and corneal scarring and ulceration.

Eye conditions in your Chihuahua are likely to be correctable, but early detection is always key.

Glaucoma

Glaucoma is caused by intraocular pressure (pressure within your dog's eyeball), and is extremely painful. Most often this disease is congenital, but can also be associated with a coexisting disease. In rare cases a luxating (floating) cataract can block the natural fluid drainage of a dog's eye, causing glaucoma. Symptoms of glaucoma include redness, cloudiness, tearing, loss of vision, an enlarged eyeball, unusual aggressiveness, lethargy, and loss of appetite. Glaucoma is considered an ophthalmic emergency—permanent vision loss can result in mere hours if severe pressure isn't relieved.

Progressive Retinal Atrophy/Degeneration

Progressive retinal atrophy (PRA) and progressive retinal degeneration (PRD) are inherited disorders in which the dog's retina deteriorates or atrophies (shrinks) over time. Though not painful, neither condition is currently treatable, but sight loss is usually gradual. If you notice your dog bumping into objects in

Living With a Blind Dog

Many blind dogs live surprisingly fulfilling and normal lives. As one veterinary ophthalmologist explained it to me, to a dog the world is really so much more about its other senses. Certainly vision loss demands adjustment from both the dog and his owner, but it is not nearly as horrific as many owners fear. If your Chihuahua is already vision impaired or within the stages of gradual sight loss, there are many wonderful resources available in bookstores and on the Internet that can answer many common questions about canine blindness.

If you suspect that your Chihuahua is experiencing vision problems, ask your veterinarian to suggest a canine ophthalmologist, or contact the British Veterinary Association at www.bva.co.uk for a referral.

dimly lit rooms, this may be an early warning sign of PRA or PRD. Other symptoms include dilated pupils and shininess or hyperreflectivity to the back of the eye, but unfortunately these symptoms are not always noticeable until the disease has reached an advanced stage.

If your Chihuahua is diagnosed with an eye disease, don't despair. In many cases correction is possible. If your dog has never had an eye exam, you might want to schedule an appointment as a preventive measure even if everything seems okay. Just like any other disease, early detection can be key in preventing progression in many instances. If left undiagnosed, and therefore untreated, your Chihuahua could lose his eyesight permanently.

OTHER HEALTH ISSUES YOUR CHIHUAHUA MAY FACE

Allergies

Allergies are relatively common in pets. Just like people, many dogs suffer from food allergies. Also similar to the problem in humans, identifying canine allergens can be rather time consuming. Although allergy tests are available, often the most effective route is good old-fashioned trial and error. If your Chihuahua's tummy seems to be consistently upset by his food, begin removing as few ingredients at once as possible (ideally just one at a time) and watching for any physical reactions. If no improvement is noticed after several days, return that item to your dog's diet and remove another, until you can isolate the problem-causing agent. Common canine food allergens are maize and wheat, but since every dog is different, the problem could be literally anything. The best way to avoid this painstaking identification process is to introduce new foods to your dog slowly, and one at a time.

Other common canine allergies involve skin reactions. Sometimes smaller breeds are prone to skin problems related to allergies, but regular grooming (especially brushing) can help prevent these issues. Bear in mind, however, that bathing too frequently (or without a shampoo created to help a particular problem) can often aggravate a skin irritation. If your Chihuahua experiences severe itching, redness, or a rash, schedule an appointment with your veterinarian to determine the cause. Make note of when the problem first appeared and any other symptoms your dog may also have, as this information may help your vet in diagnosing the problem.

Bacterial/Viral Infections

Distemper

Distemper is among the deadliest of canine viruses, killing approximately 50 percent of the adult dogs that it infects. In puppies this mortality rate is closer to 80 percent. Distemper may be spread through a number of different mediums, including saliva, urine and faeces, and even airborne matter expelled through coughing and sneezing.

Small dogs like the Chihuahua may be prone to skin allergies.

Perhaps the scariest part of distemper is that it does not affect every dog in the same way. Dogs with poor immune systems may succumb to the virus and its serious secondary infections, whereas other more resilient dogs may exhibit few symptoms or even none at all. Because distemper may be misdiagnosed in its early stages as an upper respiratory infection, owners have to remain vigilant. If your unvaccinated dog's eyes or nose secrete a thick yellow discharge, or if your dog develops a dry cough, the problem may be distemper. Diarrhoea or vomiting may also be among the symptoms.

Although distemper is viral in nature,

it can seriously compromise your dog's immune system, leaving him extremely vulnerable to a variety of bacterial infections. If left untreated, distemper can progress into pneumonia or neurological problems, including encephalitis, partial paralysis, or seizures.

The best way to prevent this virus is vaccination. Treatment for distemper depends largely on how the virus has affected an individual dog, but may include fluids, antibiotics, anti-convulsants, or sedatives. Whichever kind of treatment is necessary, one thing is certain—prevention is highly preferred.

Kennel Cough

Kennel cough is another easily avoided problem, but one far less severe in most cases than either distemper or parvovirus. It affects unvaccinated dogs with a dry persistent cough, runny eyes and nose, and occasionally even swollen tonsils. An infected dog may also seem lethargic and lose its appetite.

If the problem is viral, treatment with medication is not necessary; the problem should subside within two to three weeks on its own. If the problem is bacterial, your veterinarian may recommend treatment with antibiotics. In either case, the coughing will likely leave your Chihuahua unusually thirsty, so make sure your dog's bowl remains full of fresh water throughout the recovery period.

Parvo

Discovered in the 1970s, parvovirus is another of the deadliest viruses among dogs. It menacingly attacks the gastrointestinal tract and is then spread through contaminated faeces. Because it has the ability to survive in the environment for several months, parvo can be tracked into the home on anyone's shoes, and be left to attack the next unvaccinated puppy to come in contact with it. Resistant to most household disinfectants, parvo can only be eradicated from your household surfaces by a thorough cleaning with bleach.

As with distemper, the most effective means of preventing parvovirus is vaccination. Once parvo hits, it wreaks its havoc quickly. For this reason, vaccination is particularly important for

Chihuahuas are not prone to cancer, but you still should keep an eye out for suspicious lumps or bumps.

young dogs, as the virus can kill puppies within as little as 48 hours. Entire litters have been wiped out with the onset of parvovirus.

Signs of parvo include lethargy, loss of appetite, and vomiting. This is followed by a high fever and persistent, bloody diarrhoea within just 24 hours. Parvo should be treated with fluids and antibiotics immediately. A test to identify the virus should also be performed, but treatment must begin even before the results are available. Timing is the biggest factor for a positive prognosis.

Cancer

Fortunately, the Chihuahua is not a cancer-prone breed. It is important to note that when this diagnosis is made, though, the word "cancer" no longer has the bleak connotation it once did. The disease most frequently strikes dogs over the age of 10, but a dog of any age or breed can be stricken with cancer, and more importantly, can beat it.

Mast cell tumours, one of the most common cancers in dogs, can frequently be removed with great success. Having your dog spayed may prevent mammary tumours, the most common kind of cancer in female dogs. Similarly, testicular cancer can be prevented in males by neutering.

Common Mites

Demodex mite:	Visible only through a microscope, lives inside hair follicles
Harvest mite:	Visible in autumn as a red dot, commonly called a chigger
Cheyletiella mite:	Highly contagious, resembles a flake of walking dandruff
Sarcoptes mite:	Causes severe itching, prefers ear tips and elbows

Always be on the lookout for any suspicious looking lumps or bumps on your Chihuahua. Most will end up being benign, but you can literally save your dog's life by just giving him a quick once-over whenever you groom or pet your pooch, and following up with your veterinarian on anything out of the ordinary. Early detection is crucial.

Ear Infections and Mites

Although extremely rare in Chihuahuas due to their pricked ears, ear infections can cause serious damage when overlooked. Typically, a dog suffering from an ear infection will tilt his head to one side, scratch at the ear, or shake his head from discomfort. The infected ear will often look red inside and may also have an unpleasant odour. If you suspect that your Chihuahua has an ear infection, schedule an appointment with your dog's veterinarian. Ear infections do not go away without the treatment of an antibiotic.

Mites, tiny crab-like parasites, can infest a dog's ear causing symptoms amazingly similar to those of an ear infection. Unlike an ear infection, though, the itching and irritation caused by mites often spreads to other areas of an affected dog's body, including his back, neck, and tail. Mites are also highly contagious to other dogs within the household, as well as humans.

If mites are present, your Chihuahua may have a thick, crusty, black ear discharge. It is likely that you won't be able to discern an ear infection from a mite infestation, though, without the help of your veterinarian, who will be able to easily identify either problem and prescribe the appropriate antibiotic needed for treatment.

Epilepsy

While it does not top the list of diseases specific to the Chihuahua, epilepsy is one of the most common neurological diseases in dogs. Whether attacks occur just occasionally or frequently, they can be highly stressful events for both dog and owner. Caused by an abnormality of electrical impulses in the brain, epilepsy presents itself in the form of seizures. A minor seizure may cause your Chihuahua to only lose some of his motor control. A more serious seizure can cause a dog to fall to the floor, convulse uncontrollably, and even lose control of his bowels or bladder. The disease most often strikes animals between the ages of one and five years old. In these cases genetics are most likely the culprit. When an older dog experiences these symptoms, the cause is usually another more serious disease.

Make sure your Chihuahua gets adequate exercise to help protect him from obesity.

If present at the time of a seizure, an owner should pay close attention to everything that happens, including what was happening before the seizure began. Also, note the date, time, and length of the episode. Even in dogs that experience frequent seizures, it is highly unlikely that your veterinarian will ever be there at the time of an epileptic episode, so an owner's observations can be very important. If your Chihuahua ever experiences a seizure, try to remain as calm as possible. Your dog should be examined after the episode. (Seizures lasting longer than a minute or two require immediate veterinary attention.) If your dog is not beset with frequent seizures, medication may not be necessary, but there are anticonvulsant medications available for more serious cases.

Hip Dysplasia

One of the most common problems seen by veterinarians, hip dysplasia affects dogs of all ages and breeds. It is also an extremely common cause of arthritis. Hip dysplasia occurs when there is a deformity of the ball and socket joint in the animal's hip. Like a square peg being forced into a round hole, the joint continually grinds as the dog walks.

Signs include apparent discomfort both during and after rigorous exercise, lameness first thing in the morning, and walking with an altered gait, sometimes to the point of hopping. Hip dysplasia

is caused by genetic factors, but can be negatively affected by such environmental dynamics as poor diet, lack of exercise, and excess weight. Since keeping your dog fit can be beneficial—but impact can be a problem—swimming is an excellent form of exercise. Keeping your dog warm and away from drafts can also help. Certain dietary supplements, such as glucosamine and chondroitin, are commonly used with frequent success. Employing a canine physical therapist is often recommended for dogs with this issue.

Impacted Anal Sacs

If your Chihuahua is dragging his bottom across the floor, he is probably suffering from impacted anal sacs. There are sacs lined with glands on either side of your Chihuahua's anal opening. Usually these sacs empty themselves every time your dog defecates, but they can fill with fluid if the sacs don't empty themselves naturally. Impacted anal glands can be very uncomfortable for your dog.

If your Chihuahua is experiencing a problem, your veterinarian can empty your dog's anal sacs. Although it can be a rather unpleasant job due to odour, some groomers also provide this service. If not emptied, impacted anal glands can become infected and even rupture.

Obesity

One serious medical problem that is often overlooked is canine obesity. Extra weight adds extra stress to your dog's heart, lungs, liver, and kidneys, and places him at higher risk for various kinds of diseases and injuries. Obese dogs even suffer from weakened immune systems, making them more vulnerable to both viral and bacterial infections. To help protect your Chihuahua from becoming overweight, be conservative when dispensing even nutritious treats, and make sure your dog gets adequate exercise.

As a dog gains weight, his owner may gradually lose sight of what is a normal, healthy weight. Since just a small amount of weight on a Chihuahua can make such a huge difference, it is wise to keep an eye on the scale. Individual weights may vary slightly, but your veterinarian can tell you what is ideal for your dog. Generally, a dog shouldn't gain any more than 15 percent of his normally healthy adult body weight. Regularly check your dog's ribs—you should be able to feel them just under the skin.

Natural Flea Remedies

Natural and environmentally friendly products are available for treating both animals and their environments. Herbal alternatives containing no pesticides can be purchased in such forms as collars, sprays, and shampoos. These organic treatments repel fleas rather than kill them. For this reason, flea trapping devices should be used in conjunction with these methods. In addition to using natural repellents, such as citronella and eucalyptus, natural products may also include ingredients to strengthen your dog's immune system, since unhealthy dogs can possess an increased risk of contracting fleas and other parasites.

If your Chihuahua has fleas, remember to treat your home as well as your dog.

Parasites

Some of the most preventable canine illnesses are those caused by internal and external parasites.

Fleas

Fleas can attack dogs virtually anytime and anywhere, subjecting your Chihuahua to considerably more than a little bit of itching. For every flea you find on your dog, there will be plenty more developing in your home. Most dogs are allergic to flea saliva that is left on their skin once biting begins; some will scratch to the point of creating sores and skin infection. If left untreated, fleas can cause serious illness, including anaemia and the transmission of tapeworms. In the case of severe infestation on a puppy or debilitated dog, death can result. Even if your Chihuahua is primarily an indoor dog, he is still at risk of infestation if not treated with a regular preventative.

The family cat can carry in enough fleas to make your dog equally miserable. Since fleas can survive for as long as it takes to eradicate them, your pets can even suffer during colder months. Since fleas thrive in warm temperatures, your home is the perfect place for fleas to set up house; they can easily hide in such places as carpets, furniture, and even draperies. It doesn't matter if yours is the cleanest house in the neighbourhood; fleas don't discriminate.

Heartworm Fact

Once in the dog's heart, the worms can grow to as long as 14 inches (35.6 cm) and cause significant damage to the heart, lungs, and other vital organs. If left untreated, heartworm disease can result in death.

Heartworm is only a problem if you are taking your dog overseas. If so, contact your vet for advice on preventative care.

They will feed off any host they can find—your dog, your cat, and even human family members.

Capable of jumping 13 inches (33 cm) or more horizontally, fleas can be difficult to locate and catch, but constant itching is the most reliable sign of their presence. They also tend to favour certain areas on dogs, including near the ears, on the neck and abdomen, and around the base of the tail.

An easy way to do a flea check on your dog is using a comb. Gently run the comb through your Chihuahua's coat, and then shake any matter left on the comb onto a moistened piece of white paper or tissue. If this foreign matter begins to dissolve, leaving a red stain, your Chihuahua probably has fleas. (The red colour is caused by ingested blood in the fleas' faeces.)

Preventative treatments recommended by your veterinarian are the safest and most effective route for combating fleas. Administered once a month, the majority of these topical solutions are applied to a small area of the dog's skin. The solutions then spread progressively over the skin's surface, ridding your dog of his current fleas within hours and also preventing future infestation. These medications must be prescribed by a veterinarian who will provide you with detailed instructions on application after deciding on an appropriate dosage for your Chihuahua.

If your Chihuahua has fleas, see your veterinarian as soon as possible. Also, remember to treat the environment, as well as your dog. Flea bombs, also called foggers, can help rid this nuisance from your home, but check with your veterinarian before deciding on a plan of attack. (If your dog spends time outdoors, also ask about treating your garden.) Because you are dealing with highly toxic chemicals, carefully read labels and follow directions thoroughly. Most importantly, remember to remove all people and pets from the home before treating it. If your home is carpeted, make sure to vacuum repeatedly after a flea infestation and dispose of the bag immediately whether it is full or not.

Check with your veterinarian before using any over-the-counter flea or tick product. Organophosphate insecticides (OPs) and carbamates are found in various products and should be avoided, as they pose particular health threats to children and pets even when used correctly. A product contains an OP if the ingredient list contains chlorpyrifos, dichlorvos, phosmet, naled, tetrachlorvinphos, diazinon, or malathion. The product contains a carbamate if the ingredient list includes carbaryl or propoxur.

Heartworm

Mosquitoes are carriers of the heartworm, a parasite that can cause your Chihuahua weeks of uncomfortable treatment, and in advanced cases can take his life. Although many people erroneously believe that heartworm is only a threat to dogs in warm climates, the larval development of the mosquito species that serve as intermediate hosts for this disease can occur in temperatures as low as 57°F (13.9°C).

Heartworm is not currently found in the UK. However, if you are travelling abroad with your Chihuahua you will need to see your veterinarian about a preventative before you go.

If your dog tests positive for heartworm, treatment must be started at

Holistic medicine can be a valuable part of your Chihuahua's health care.

once. Symptoms of heartworm disease include coughing, exercise intolerance, and abnormal lung sounds; however, a blood test is often the very first indicator. Treating the disease can be an extremely complicated and expensive procedure with serious side effects. When caught early, successful treatment of this devastating illness is possible, but prevention is highly preferred.

Other Worms

Other parasites that may infest your Chihuahua are commonly referred to as worms. Although the presence of certain types (such as roundworms and tapeworms) can easily be seen in your dog's stool, diagnosing others (such as whipworms and hookworms) can be more difficult. Signs of worms include excessive licking of the anal region or dragging the rear end.

Since several of these parasites can also infest humans, it is especially important to prevent them from attacking your dog in the first place. Keep your garden free of canine faeces, since soil contamination from excrement creates ideal conditions for many of

Your Chihuahua's First-Aid Kit

The following items should always be kept on hand in the event of a medical emergency:

- Antibiotic ointment
- Canine first-aid manual
- Children's diphenhydramine (antihistamine)
- Syrup
- Cotton swabs
- Emergency phone numbers (including emergency veterinarian, and your dog's regular vet)
- Flashlight
- Hydrogen peroxide
- Instant ice pack
- Ipecac syrup
- Mineral oil
- Nonstick gauze pads, gauze, and tape
- Oral syringe or eyedropper
- Rectal thermometer
- Saline solution
- Scissors
- Silver nitrate stick
- Soap
- Styptic powder or pencil
- Tweezers
- Any other item your veterinarian recommends keeping on hand

these worms. As an added precaution, always bring along a stool sample when visiting the veterinarian, so a closer look under the microscope can be made.

Never give your Chihuahua a wormer (medication intended to rid a dog's body of worms) without the prior approval and instruction of your vet. If your dog does become infested with worms, seek treatment at once (don't forget to bring a stool sample), and be sure to follow up by treating the dog's environment to prevent further infestation.

Ticks

If your Chihuahua spends any time outdoors, you will need to check your dog regularly for ticks. Ticks can easily leap onto your pet and hold on for dear life, putting your dog at risk for serious disease. When a tick first attaches itself to your dog's skin, it may be difficult to spot due to its minute size and typical brownish-white colouring, but once it swells with blood, an engorged tick may reach the size of a plump pea. This may still be hard to see on a long-haired dog, so you must always be on the lookout. Ticks are most prevalent in the warmer months, but they can survive in temperatures as low as 35°F (1.7°C). Combing your dog whenever he has been outdoors is an excellent way to find anything that might be hiding within his coat before it can cause a serious problem.

The deer tick, also known as the black-legged tick, is especially difficult to notice, since it is only the size of a sesame seed before becoming engorged with blood. Once it has fed, it will still only measure between 3 and 6 mm. This is the tick that gets the most media attention, as it is the best-known carrier of Lyme disease. Though not contagious, Lyme disease (named for the town in Connecticut where the first outbreak occurred) is a very serious illness for both dogs and people. Although not common in the UK, Lyme Disease is occuring more frequently.

One of the most common signs of canine Lyme disease is limping, frequently with one of the front legs. Other signs include lymph node swelling in the affected limb, and a fever. If left untreated, the disease will progress quickly, leaving the animal virtually unable to walk within just days. Treatment with an antibiotic is imperative. When caught early, permanent joint or nerve damage may be avoided.

The best way to avoid the onset of Lyme disease is by having your dog vaccinated, but you will still need to check your dog regularly, as many other types of ticks may be lurking in your own back garden. If you do find a tick on your Chihuahua, swab the tick and surrounding tissue with rubbing alcohol as you slowly pull on the tick with a pair of tweezers. It is particularly important that you approach this manoeuvre gently, since your objective is to get the tick to release its grip on your dog; this will ensure that no part of the tick is left behind in your dog's skin. If the head remains embedded, bring your dog to a veterinarian for its complete removal.

Ticks can be hard to spot at first, but become engorged with blood and grow larger after feeding.

Remember to save the portion of the tick you were able to remove, as this may be helpful to your veterinarian in identifying it. If you feel more comfortable having your vet handle the removal from the very beginning, by all means bring your dog to the surgery as soon as you discover the tick's presence.

Rocky Mountain spotted fever, ehrlichiosis (a bacterial infection), and babesiosis (a blood disorder) are just a few of the dangerous illnesses ticks can transmit. Although there is no universal vaccine to prevent all the diseases caused by ticks, treating your dog with a regular preventive flea and tick medication can significantly reduce your dog's risk of unwittingly playing host to these dangerous creatures. You will also be protecting your human family from the many tick-transmitted illnesses that can endanger their health, as well.

Reaction to Anaesthesia

There is always a certain amount of risk associated with anaesthesia. For this reason preventive health care is preferred to having your dog anaesthetised—regular teeth brushing, for example, instead of a veterinary dental cleaning. In the past, toy breeds have faced particular dangers relating to anaesthesia, but newer inhalant anaesthetics have lowered these risks significantly.

Whenever possible, it is a good idea to postpone elective procedures until your dog needs to be anaesthetised for another, more pressing reason.

Also, you can lower your dog's risks by having your vet run blood tests before any surgery. One of the biggest factors is your Chihuahua's weight. Obese dogs face significantly higher risks due to anaesthesia. Owners of overweight dogs often find themselves having to put off even medically necessary operations until the dog loses enough weight to make the use of anaesthesia a safe undertaking.

COMPLEMENTARY MEDICINE

Years ago, treatments such as acupuncture and chiropractic were unheard of in the veterinary field, but these complementary therapies are now being offered and used regularly throughout the veterinary world. Once labelled alternative medicine, holistic approaches are no longer considered mutually exclusive choices from conventional care. They are valuable parts of a comprehensive system, as well as legitimate modalities in their own right. Derived from the word "whole", the term "holistic medicine" encompasses a group of ancient techniques that treat the mind, body, and spirit—not just the more apparent, physical symptoms of an illness.

Anaesthesia and Obesity

An overweight dog is in serious danger of complications when undergoing anaesthesia, and medical procedures may need to be delayed until the dog loses enough weight to be safely anaesthetised. This is just one of many reasons to closely monitor your dog's diet and exercise level to prevent obesity.

Acupuncture and Chiropractic

Acupuncture, an ancient Chinese method of healing, involves the insertion of fine needles into various parts of the body to stimulate good health. Veterinary acupuncture may be used to treat such problems as arthritis, epilepsy, and even cancer. In many cases it has been shown to relieve pain, improve organ functioning, and strengthen the immune system. Though the process may seem intimidating to some owners, most dogs find the process completely painless.

Chiropractic focuses on the spine and joints, manipulating them through careful adjustments to alleviate pain and improve the general health of the animal. Like acupuncturists, veterinary chiropractors do not diagnose disease. They identify and correct vertebral subluxations—dislocations of the bones or joints surrounding the spinal column that may be hindering the animal's health.

Veterinary acupuncturists and chiropractors should be certified by the Association of British Veterinary Accupuncture (ABVA), the Veterinary College of Chiropractic or the Oxford College of Chiropractic (formerly the Witney School of Chiropractic). You should also use the same level of scrutiny in selecting either individual as you would in choosing a veterinarian.

Homeopathy

Homeopathy is another element of ancient holistic medicine that your veterinarian, acupuncturist, or chiropractor may suggest. A large part of homeopathic medicine is based on the use of substances that actually produce symptoms of the disease the veterinary caregiver is trying to cure. Diluted to infinitesimal doses in solutions, the tenet of this practice is that the smaller the dose, the more powerful the effect. After a homeopathic treatment, your dog may experience a temporary intensification of symptoms (an even higher fever, for instance), but the ultimate goal is creating a natural resistance to the disease or illness. Although the concept is somewhat similar to vaccination, homeopathic medicines are far removed from the pharmacologic doses employed in vaccines.

Massage Therapy

Canine massage is used in various types of complementary medicine, but it is also a relaxing technique that, with a small amount of instruction, can be performed by a dog owner at home on a more basic level. Providing both a Chihuahua and his owner with special one-on-one time, massage can be an amazing stress reducer for your dog. Touch feels good and offers several health benefits, including increased circulation, relief of muscle tension, relaxation of muscle spasms, and increased range of motion. Massaging your dog can even lower your own blood pressure.

The Tellington TTouch is a well-known form of animal massage therapy. Created by Linda Tellington-Jones in 1978, this technique

You may want to use a combination of traditional and complementary medical treatments for your dog.

that uses various types of touches, lifts, and movement exercise is now used throughout the world. It has been extremely effective in correcting behaviour problems (such as aggression and chewing), improving quality of life for ageing pets, and even helping with carsickness.

You should never perform canine massage or any other kind of complementary medicine without proper instruction from a qualified provider. Similarly, always remember that no procedure should ever be used as a substitute for licensed veterinary care. There are many good books and videos available about the use of canine massage in the home. Your dog's reaction is the most important thing. Even if you are doing everything right, if your Chihuahua shows any signs of displeasure, stop the massage immediately. Most dogs will enjoy being massaged, but just like a human being, every dog is different.

Just because a certain treatment works well for one dog or affliction, it doesn't necessarily mean it will work for every dog or every situation. Results may also take time. Beware of any provider who doesn't take the time to evaluate your animal completely. All factors (both physical and emotional) that may be contributing to your dog's problem must be considered; this is the very basis of the holistic approach. Holistic medicine is not a panacea, but it may offer additional options for improving your Chihuahua's health.

Physical Therapy

Modern physical therapy is barely a century old, the canine application even younger, but like holistic medicine, many of the agents employed in this modality have actually been utilised since ancient times. In addition to more technological tools such as ultrasound and electrical stimulation, a canine physical therapist may use massage, therapeutic exercise, and hydrotherapy (water) to help dogs suffering from such afflictions as cruciate ligament problems, hip dysplasia, and spinal injuries.

Although all veterinarians are legally able to perform physical therapy, typically very few receive physical therapy training as a part of their education. An ideal caregiver is an individual who is both a veterinarian and a licensed physical therapist. If you have trouble finding such an individual, look for a physical therapist

Keeping Calm in an Emergency

In an emergency situation, giving in to panic not only can add to your dog's anxiety but also can cause you to act rashly and perhaps even worsen the situation. Remaining calm is one of the most important things you can do in a medical emergency.

who is willing to work together with your Chihuahua's veterinarian.

EMERGENCY FIRST AID

If your Chihuahua is involved in a medical emergency, the most important thing for you to do is remain calm. Not only can rash actions spurred by anxiety make your dog's situation even worse, but also, animals possess an uncanny ability to sense a human's nervousness. You can unintentionally scare your Chihuahua if you don't pay attention to your own verbal and physical reactions. Bring your dog to the closest veterinarian immediately, calling to let the surgery know you are on your way if possible. Also, depending on the type of emergency, there may be things you can do to help ensure a positive outcome.

A dog's body is very different from a person's in many ways. For this reason canine first aid differs dramatically from our human perceptions of emergency care. Medical doctors are taught very early in their careers that the first rule of medicine is to do no harm. This is also excellent advice for all dog owners. Never give your dog any medication without first checking with your veterinarian. Drugs that can help people, such as acetaminophen and ibuprofen, can be fatal for animals. Also, procedures such as the Heimlich manoeuvre need to be performed very differently on a choking Chihuahua than on a 200-pound (90.7 kg) man.

Canine CPR

CPR stands for cardiopulmonary resuscitation, a combination of rescue breathing and chest compressions delivered to victims of cardiac arrest. This technique that is regularly used on humans can also be used on animals in similar emergency situations. The worst time to learn canine CPR, however, is during an emergency. You can ask your veterinarian if there are any organisations in your area that offer courses in canine CPR. If your Chihuahua is not breathing and you do not know how to perform canine CPR, bring the dog to a veterinarian at once.

Choking

Choking may have a number of possible causes, including any small object that can get lodged in your Chihuahua's trachea. Choking is a veterinary emergency, and immediate assistance is necessary. An animal that is choking may drool, gag, struggle to breathe, paw at his face, and regurgitate.

If you think your Chihuahua is choking, first remove his collar (if present), and then examine the inside of the dog's mouth. It is very important that you do not simply pull on any object you may feel in your dog's throat, as dogs have small bones that support the base of their tongues that can easily be mistaken for the object in question. If you cannot identify or remove the object, lift your Chihuahua up with his head pointing downwards. This might dislodge the object.

If this doesn't work, you will need to perform a modified Heimlich manoeuvre. Holding the dog around his waist so his bottom is closest to you, place a fist just behind the ribs. Compress the abdomen several times (begin with three) with quick upward pressure, and again check the mouth. Even if you are able to dislodge the object and your dog appears fine, it is a good idea to see your veterinarian immediately in case of any internal injury. This is especially important due to your Chihuahua's size.

Knowledge of canine CPR can save your dog's life in an emergency.

Cuts

Lacerations to paws and pads are among the most common canine injuries. If your Chihuahua experiences a serious cut, apply a gauze pad soaked in cold water to the wound, and then contact your veterinarian. Do not use absorbent cotton, as it can adhere to the cut and leave fibres in the wound.

If blood is spurting from the wound, the dog has most likely severed an artery and needs to be taken to a veterinary surgery immediately. Applying firm pressure over the wet gauze pad should stop minor bleeding. Silver nitrate sticks are also useful for speeding the clotting process. To prevent debris from contaminating the wound, flush it with wound cleaning solution, saline solution, or plain water before covering. Once the bleeding has stopped and the laceration has been cleaned, cover the wound with a nonstick pad and secure it with a bandage.

Encounters With Other Animals and Insects

Bites

Bites from other animals require prompt veterinary attention. This is especially important for a Chihuahua, as even a small bite from another animal can be catastrophic to this toy breed. Also, never assume that a neighbourhood dog's vaccinations are current. Even if the owner assures you that they are, getting your dog to his vet as quickly as possible will help ensure the best positive outcome.

If a wild animal (such as a fox) bites your Chihuahua, your dog will need to be taken to the vet immediately.

Stings

Insect stings can be extremely dangerous. Bee and wasp stings in particular can cause very quick and severe reactions, but these effects are even more rapid in small dogs. If your Chihuahua is stung, call your veterinarian at once. Ice can help reduce swelling; a swollen muzzle is often an indication of a bee sting. Keep some children's diphenhydramine (a common antihistamine used to treat

If your Chihuahua has an encounter with a wild animal, be sure to take him to the vet for immediate care.

allergic reactions) on hand, and ask your vet for the correct dosage for your dog. This medicine could save your dog's life if he experiences a severe reaction to an insect sting.

Dehydration and Heatstroke

Dehydration and heatstroke are usually highly preventable problems. Although your Chihuahuas may love the sun, pay attention to your local weather report and any warnings of especially dangerous times to be outdoors. Since dogs only have sweat glands on the pads of their feet, they cannot lose heat through sweating like humans. Instead, they pant—the first sign that they need water and shelter from the heat. Remember, if you feel hot and thirsty, most likely your dog does, too. Always provide plenty of fresh drinking water for your Chihuahua when spending time outside, and stay inside on especially stifling days.

If you suspect that your Chihuahua is suffering from heatstroke, place the dog in a tub of cool water or gently wrap him in a towel soaked with cold water. Never use ice-cold water. Once your dog's temperature is lowered to 103°F (39.4°C) (a rectal thermometer can provide you with an accurate reading), seek veterinary care at once.

Eye Injuries

Eye injuries require prompt veterinary care. Abrasions, lacerations, or punctures to the eye will cause your dog to keep the eye tightly closed, so you will unlikely be able to do much to help the dog yourself. If your dog has something stuck in his eye, you may try flushing the area with irrigation fluid or saline solution, but still contact your veterinarian. The vet can tell if the object has caused any scratching of the cornea. If a chemical irritant was involved in the injury, flush the eye as much as possible yourself, and bring the dog to your veterinarian as quickly as possible. If both eyes seem to be affected, a chemical irritant is likely the cause of the problem.

Poison

When we think of dangerous canine poisons, a handful of obvious substances stand out among the rest. Chocolate, certain houseplants, and many human medications all certainly top the list of toxic substances that should never be given to dogs, but we must also remember that poisons don't always have to be swallowed to pose a problem. Toxins can be eaten, inhaled, or absorbed by a

dog's skin—sometimes even without an owner's knowledge.

When a previously healthy dog becomes suddenly ill with no apparent explanation, poisoning is frequently suspected. Signs of poisoning may include vomiting, diarrhoea, and trembling, but many chemical toxins do not trigger distinctive signs of illness. This makes identification of the toxin nearly impossible in most cases. If you have reason to believe that your dog has been exposed to any kind of poison, seek advice from a qualified professional immediately.

Ipecac syrup can readily induce vomiting, but depending on the type of poisoning this might not be prudent. Caustic toxins, such as drain cleaner, can burn the throat a second time when brought back up through the oesophagus. If there is any question as to what kind of poison your dog has ingested, wait for instructions from an expert before doing anything.

Trauma

If your dog experiences trauma, a severe injury or shock to the body from a fall or other accident, you will need to get your dog to a veterinarian as soon as possible. Extreme care needs to be used when moving an injured animal, but in order to help your dog you must first protect yourself. Injured animals can act aggressively when they are experiencing trauma, and they may not even recognise their beloved owners. You should never get too close to an injured animal's face. Chihuahuas may be little, but they can deliver a serious bite nonetheless, especially when in pain themselves.

Check for obvious injuries such as bleeding or distorted limbs. If an appendage is bleeding profusely, a rubber band can serve as a makeshift tourniquet in an emergency. If a bone appears to be fractured or broken, use care not to handle it when moving the animal. Very gently move the dog onto a stiff surface, such as a board, if possible. Use this as an impromptu stretcher. A blanket or a coat will suffice if nothing else is available. If you are alone and cannot hold the dog in place, use a belt or rope to secure him for the ride to the veterinary surgery. Use rolled towels or another coat to keep the dog warm and prevent him from moving around. Keep the dog as still as possible.

GERIATRIC CARE

Early preventive care will help ensure that your Chihuahua lives a long, enjoyable life, but even the healthiest dogs face specific challenges as they age. The old claim that one dog year equals seven human years has been refuted many times. Smaller breeds in particular surpass this outdated comparison. While larger breeds such as Great Danes have a shorter lifespan, Chihuahuas and other toy breeds can live well into their teens. As your dog gets older, prevention continues to be his best defence against serious conditions that can interfere with his longevity.

Just like people, healthy pets tend to age more slowly than those who lead unhealthy lifestyles.

If a nutritious diet and exercise are part of your Chihuahua's daily life, he will likely act youthful for a long time. Likewise even a young dog can appear elderly if not kept in proper health. There are no guarantees that disease will not befall a well cared for dog, but preventive care will help his chances with whatever might lie ahead.

Problems Your Older Chihuahua May Face

Like people, older dogs often show signs of their years. The coat of a mature Chihuahua will become thinner and drier as he ages, and hair around the face and ears will turn grey. The lenses in the eyes may become cloudy with a blue-grey appearance. In addition to the aesthetic signs of ageing, your dog's hearing will deteriorate as he ages, sometimes resulting in total deafness.

Heart, liver, and kidney functioning tend to become less efficient as dogs age. The immune system is also less able to fight off bacteria and viruses. Occasionally, incontinence can become an issue. For these reasons, owners of older Chihuahuas should increase the frequency of regular veterinary checkups to twice a year. Your vet may also suggest adding blood tests to the routine at this time to monitor various organ functioning.

Extra TLC

Your veteran Chihuahua needs extra love and care to help him through his golden years. Beware of potential aches and pains that didn't show before. Make sure he is eating right and getting enough exercise—and rest!

You want him to be comfortable as he lives out his days.

Arthritis

You may notice your Chihuahua starting to slow down a bit physically after the age of seven. This will usually be most apparent when your dog moves from lying down to standing or when walking up stairs, but it might also be noticeable during cold, damp weather. Slowing movement is a chronic sign of arthritis, one of the most common afflictions among elderly dogs.

There are many different medications available to ease the pain of arthritis, but careful diagnosis is imperative. Literally the inflammation of a joint, arthritis can strike at any age—particularly after an injury in an area where scar tissue may be present. Arthritis is more common in overweight dogs, but can also occur as a result of genetics, targeting an animal's weakest areas. For the Chihuahua, this vulnerable area might be the knees.

There are many different medications available to ease the pain of arthritis, but first careful diagnosis is imperative. Once your veterinarian has established that your dog is indeed suffering from arthritis (with the use of x-rays), he or she may prescribe an anti-inflammatory medication. Certain dietary supplements may also be recommended, particularly glucosamine and chondroitin. Acupuncture has been found helpful in many cases.

You will be instructed to help your dog lose any excess weight and incorporate a reasonable amount of exercise into his routine. This is one of the most important steps in managing this chronic condition, since lowering your dog's weight also lowers his risk for future injuries that can compound the problems of arthritis.

Patience will also be a large part of helping your arthritic Chihuahua. Once arthritis sets in, it may take your dog a little longer to get up and move. You mustn't rush an arthritic animal, as this can only make further injury more likely. Similarly, you will need to be attentive to your Chihuahua's exercise needs while making sure that your dog doesn't overdo it. These stubborn little dogs like to live life on their own terms, and they can be extremely energetic and resilient. They need you to know when it's time to say when.

Hypothyroidism

Another prevalent canine condition with similar symptoms is an endocrine disorder called hypothyroidism. A dog's thyroid consists of two butterfly-shaped lobes located on the neck. The hormone these lobes secrete is responsible for maintaining the dog's metabolism, the rate at which the body processes its nutrients. In dogs with hypothyroidism, this gland is underactive, consequently decreasing your dog's metabolism and making it easier for your animal to gain weight. Most often a dog is predisposed to hypothyroidism, and the condition is most common in larger breeds.

Giving Your Chihuahua Medication

Pills

1. With your Chihuahua sitting, gently open his mouth with one hand and drop the pill down the back of his throat with the other.

2. Hold your dog's mouth closed with his head pointed upwards until he swallows and licks his lips, then praise the dog extensively.

Hint: If your dog is especially resistant to taking pills, you may try hiding the pill in a small piece of meat, bread, or cheese. Check with your vet first, though, since some medications should not be given with certain foods.

Liquids

Using a liquid syringe, expel the medication into the side of your dog's mouth, holding it closed immediately afterwards until swallowed.

Hint: Occasionally offer your dog a liquid treat (such as a small amount of melted ice cream) from the syringe when the dog is healthy. This will help encourage your dog to readily take medication this way when he is sick.

Injections

1. After preparing the syringe, lift the fold of skin on the scruff of your Chihuahua's neck.

2. Insert the needle sideways into the skin, being careful not to come out the other side. Empty the syringe. This approach will help you avoid hitting muscle.

Note: Injections should only be administered at home at the instruction of your dog's veterinarian.

If your dog has put on some weight, you must not assume that the thyroid gland is the cause of the problem. If your dog's food intake has not increased along with its weight, however, you may want to look for other symptoms. Has your dog experienced any hair loss or dry skin? Does your dog always seem to be cold, seeking out warmer places to rest? Does your dog seem lethargic or depressed? Have ear infections been a problem? These are all signs that the weight gain may be related to a thyroid issue.

If you suspect that your dog is suffering from hypothyroidism, schedule an appointment with your veterinarian. Although the condition is rare in toy breeds, it can beset any dog. Most dogs will show symptoms between the ages of 4 and 10. Your vet will use a series of tests to diagnose hypothyroidism. Once diagnosed, your dog will need to take a synthetic thyroid hormone to help adjust its metabolism. Periodic blood samples will then need to be drawn to assess the effectiveness of the treatment and make any necessary adjustments.

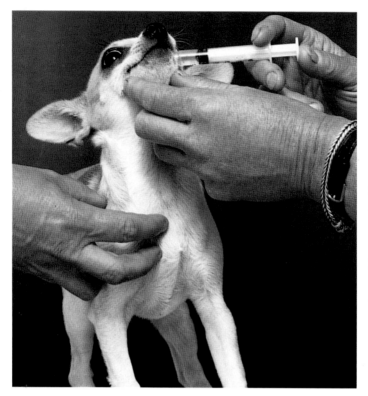

You can use a syringe to give your Chihuahua liquid medications.

Treatment is usually extremely successful. Most dogs treated for hypothyroidism return to their normal weight and activity levels quickly once treatment is begun. Although regular follow-up appointments will be necessary to monitor the hormone dosage, your dog should remain symptom-free for the rest of his life and will have the potential to live just as long as a Chihuahua without a thyroid problem.

Canine Cognitive Disorder

Similar to human Alzheimer's disease, canine cognitive disorder (CCD), also called cognitive dysfunction syndrome (CDS), can present symptoms much like those of senility. As your dog gets older, it may be more and more difficult to distinguish between CCD and the normal signs of ageing. There is one difference between the two, though, that makes differentiation especially important. Unlike senility, CCD is treatable. CCD can also affect a dog of any age, not just an elderly one.

Normal signs of ageing may include a gradual loss of mobility, reduced immune system functioning, a slowing metabolism, loss of muscle and bone mass, and reduced functioning of the senses. A dog suffering from CCD will appear less aware of his surroundings, less capable of learning or adapting, and even unable to remember simple things. Frequently, housetraining is one of the first things forgotten. In addition, CCD affects an animal's behaviour and temperament, often straining the relationship between the dog and his family.

Since CCD shares many symptoms with other common canine illnesses, your veterinarian will need to perform several tests, including blood work, urine analysis, x-rays, and a neurological examination, to rule out these other possible causes of the problem. CCD can exist alongside some of these other illnesses, making diagnosis especially challenging in these cases. There is currently no cure for CCD, but prescription medications that enhance dopamine levels in the brain can help to minimise symptoms and offer a dog a better quality of life.

Making Your Older Chihuahua Comfortable

There are several things owners can do to make their dogs' lives more comfortable as they age. If your Chihuahua's eyesight is failing or if he tends to stumble frequently, a baby gate may be useful in protecting your dog from falling down stairs. This can also protect your carpeting if your dog has become incontinent or forgetful of housetraining. If your Chihuahua doesn't already have one, an orthopaedic bed may be a good idea at this time.

Grey hairs won't bother your Chihuahua, but itchy dry skin will. To stimulate the natural oils in your dog's skin, try brushing his coat more frequently. This can also serve as an excellent opportunity to check for fleas and ticks, parasites your older dog will have a harder time fighting. Use care near any of the normal lumps or bumps your dog may have at this stage of life, as harsh bristles can hurt.

LETTING GO

Many of us share a hope for our dogs that they pass quietly and comfortably in their sleep at a ripe old age. While this happens for some dogs, the more common scenario is serious illness. Canine veterinary medicine is continuously making amazing strides, and dogs (particularly smaller ones) are living longer and longer. Our canine companions give so much of themselves to us that we must also consider their quality of life during these difficult times.

Perhaps the biggest responsibility that comes with dog ownership is deciding when it is time to stop your animal's suffering. Often referred to as putting a dog to sleep, canine euthanasia is simultaneously one of the worst choices an owner ever has to make and a uniquely compassionate option. I once asked my own veterinarian how she deals with this horrible aspect of her job. She confided to me that she feels enormously grateful that veterinary medicine gives her the ability to stop the suffering of animals when there is nothing more she or anyone else can do for them.

If properly cared for, your Chihuahua will remain your best friend for years to come.

If your Chihuahua is seriously ill, the decision of whether to euthanise your dog will be an agonizing one no matter what your choice. In this situation the best thing you can do is get all the facts from a veterinarian you trust, while taking into consideration the intensity of your dog's pain and his legitimate chance of recovery.

The death of a pet can be devastating. First, give yourself permission to grieve this very real loss. Certainly, there is no single method for dealing with grief that works for everyone, but many find it helpful to reach out to those around them. Ask your vet to recommend a support group for grieving pet owners, or look for one online or in your local newspaper. Sometimes just being able to talk about the loss of your beloved dog can help.

New Beginnings

After the loss of your Chihuahua, many people will encourage you to get another dog. You may resist the idea, believing you need more time, or you may embrace the possibility of having another animal to love right away. In either case only you can make this decision.

If you want to wait before jumping back into dog ownership, give yourself all the time you need. Likewise, if you think another dog will help ease your loneliness, also give yourself some time—at least enough to choose the right dog for you and your family.

No dog will ever replace the one you have lost, of course, but just as we can love more than one person, we often have enough love in our hearts for both the treasured companion we have lost and a new friend who may need us just as much as we need him. Go back and reread the parts of this book about selecting the best dog for you. Maybe this time around you will adopt another Chihuahua, or a different breed entirely. There are countless dogs currently in need of someone just like you. When the time is right, go find each other.

Only you can determine the right time to get another dog after the loss of your pet.

ASSOCIATIONS AND ORGANISATIONS

Breed Clubs and Kennel Clubs

American Kennel Club (AKC)
5580 Centerview Drive
Raleigh, NC 27606
Telephone: (919) 233-9767
Fax: (919) 233-3627
Email: info@akc.org
www.akc.org

British Chihuahua Club
Secretary: Mrs. Corrine Towler
Email: coriam@tiscali.co.uk
www.the-british-chihuahua-club.org.uk

Canadian Kennel Club (CKC)
89 Skyway Avenue, Suite 100
Etobicoke, Ontario M9W 6R4
Telephone: (416) 675-5511
Fax: (416) 675-6506
Email: information@ckc.ca
www.ckc.ca

Chihuahua Club of America
Secretary: Tanya Delaney
Email: Elfin987@aol.com
www.chihuahuaclubofamerica.com

The Kennel Club (UK)
1 Clarges Street
London
W1J 8AB
Telephone: 0870 606 6750
Fax: 0207 518 1058
www.thekennelclub.org.uk

United Kennel Club (UKC)
100 E. Kilgore Road
Kalamazoo, MI 49002-5584
Telephone: (269) 343-9020
Email: pbickell@ukcdogs.com
www.ukcdogs.com

Websites

British Chihuahua Club
(www.the-british-chihuahua-club.org.uk)
Including information about conformations, rescue organisations, health care, traveling abroad, and adoption, this web site is a vital resource every Chihuahua owner in the UK.

Chihuahua Club of America
(www.chihuahuaclubofamerica.com)
A complete site with referrals to breeders, educators, and rescue programs, as well as listings of national events and seminars—a great way to become involved in the world of Chihuahuas.

PUBLICATIONS

Books

Evans, J M
What If My Dog?
Interpet Publishing, 2006

Tennant, Colin
Mini Encyclopedia of Dog Training & Behaviour
Interpet Publishing, 2005

Barnes, Julia
Living With a Rescued Dog
Interpet Publishing, 2004

Evans, J M & White, Kay
Doglopaedia
Ringpress Books, 1998

Evans, J M
Book of The Bitch
Ringpress Books, 1998

Magazines

Dog World
Somerfield House
Wotton Road, Ashford
Kent, TN23 6LW
Telephone: 01233 621877
www.dogworld.co.uk

Dogs Monthly
Ascot House
High Street, Ascot,
Berkshire SL5 7JG
United Kingdom
Telephone: 0870 730 8433
E-mail: admin@rtc-associates.freeserve.co.uk
www.corsini.co.uk/dogsmonthly

Dogs Today
Town Mill, Bagshot Road
Chobham
Surrey GU24 8BZ
Telephone: 01276 858880
Email: enquiries@dogstodaymagazine.co.uk
www.dogstodaymagazine.co.uk

Kennel Gazette
1 Clarges Street
London W1 8AB
Telephone: 0870 6066750
www.thekennelclub.org.uk

K9 Magazine
21 High Street
Warsop
Nottinghamshire NG20 0AA
Telephone: 0870 0114114
Email: mail@k9magazine.com
www.k9magazine.com

Our Dogs
Our Dogs Publishing
5 Oxford Road
Station Approach
Manchester M60 1SX
www.ourdogs.co.uk

Your Dog
Roebuck House
33 Broad Street
Stamford
Lincolnshire PE9 1RB
Telephone: 01780 766199

ANIMAL WELFARE GROUPS AND RESCUE ORGANISATIONS

British Veterinary Association Animal Welfare Foundation (BVA AWF)
7 Mansfield Street
London W1G 9NQ
Telephone: 0207 6366541
Email: bva-awf@bva.co.uk
www.bvaawf.org.uk

Royal Society for the
Prevention of Cruelty to
Animals (RSPCA)
Telephone: 0870 3335 999
Fax: 0870 7530 284
www.rspca.org.uk

Scottish Society for the
Prevention of Cruelty to
Animals (SSPCA)
Braehead Mains 603
Queensferry Road
Edinburgh EH4 6EA
Telephone: 0131 3390222
Email:
enquiries@scottishspca.org
www.scottishspca.org

World Animal Net (UK)
24 Barleyfields
Didcot, Oxon OX11 OBJ
Telephone: + 44 1235 210 775
E-mail: info@worldanimal.net
www.worldanimal.net

VETERINARY AND HEALTH RESOURCES

Association of British Veterinary Accupuncturists (ABVA)
66A Easthorpe, Southwell
Nottinghamshire NG25 0HZ
www.abva.co.uk

Association of Chartered Physiotherapists Specialising in Animal Therapy (ACPAT)
52 Littleham Road
Exmouth, Devon EX8 2QJ
Telephone: 01395 270 648
www.acpat.org.uk

British Association of Homeopathic Veterinary Surgeons
Alternative Veterinary Medicine Centre
Chinham House, Stanford in the Vale, Oxfordshire, SN7 8NQ
Email: enquiries@bahvs.com
www.bahvs.com

British Association of
Veterinary Opthalmologists
(BAVO)
Email: secretary@bravo.org.uk
www.bravo.org.uk

British Small Animal
Veterinary Association
(BSAVA)
Woodrow House, 1 Telford Way
Waterwells Business Park
Quedgley, Gloucester GL2 2AB
Email:
customerservices@bsava.com
www.bsava.com

British Veterinary Association
(BVA)
7 Mansfield Street
London
W1G 9NQ
Telephone: 020 7636 6541
Fax: 020 7436 2970
E-mail: bvahq@bva.co.uk
www.bva.co.uk

British Veterinary Hospotals
Association (BHVA)
Station Bungalow
Main Road, Stockfield
Northumberland NE43 7HJ
Telephone: 07966 901619
Email: office@bvha.org.uk
www.BVHA.org.uk

Royal College of Veterinary
Surgeons (RCVS)
Belgravia House
62-64 Horseferry Road
London SW1P 2AF
Telephone: 0207 2222001
Email: admin@rcvs.org.uk
www.rcvs.org.uk

THERAPY

Pets As Therapy
3 Grange Farm Cottages
Wycombe Road, Saunderton
Princes Risborough
Buckinghamshire HP27 9NS
Telephone: 0870 9770003
www.petsastherapy.org

Therapy Dogs International
(TDI)
88 Bartley Road, Flanders, NJ
07836
Telephone: (973) 2529800
email: tdi@gti.net
www.tdi-dog.org

SPORTS

Agility Club UK
www.agilityclub.co.uk

British Flyball Association
PO Box 109
Petersfield GU32 1XZ
Telephone: 01753 620110
Email: bfa@flyball.org.uk
www.flyball.org.uk

Canine Freestyle Federation Inc.
Email: secretary@canine-freestyle.org
www.canine-freestyle.org

World Canine Freestyle Organisation
PO Box 350122 Brooklyn
NY 112352525
www.worldcaninefreestyle.org

TRAINING AND BEHAVIOUR

Association of Pet Behaviour Counsellors (APBC)
PO Box 46
Worcester, WR8 9YS
Telephone: 01386 750743
Email: info@apbc.org.uk
www.apbc.org.uk

Association of Pet Dog Trainers (APDT)
PO Box 17
Kempsford, GL7 4W7
Telephone: 01285 810811
E-mail: APDoffice@aol.com
www.apdt.co.uk

For Jonathan

ACKNOWLEDGEMENTS

The author would like to thank the following people for sharing their valuable experiences and insights with her: Lynnie Bunten, National Rescue Chairperson; Lavonne Cottingham, Breeder; Carolyn Mooney, Retired AKC judge; Pat Reginer, Breeder; Donna Stitz, Breeder

ABOUT THE AUTHOR

Tammy Gagne is a freelance writer who specialises in the health and behaviour of companion animals. She is a regular contributor to several national pet care magazines and has owned purebred dogs for more than 25 years. In addition to being an avid dog lover, she is also an experienced aviculturist. She resides in northern New England with her husband, son, dogs, and parrots.

PHOTO CREDITS

Photos on p. 113, 118, 165 courtesy of Annette (Shutterstock)

Photo on p. 182 courtesy of Chris Bence (Shutterstock)

Photo on p. 168 courtesy of Melissa Bouyounan (Shutterstock)

Photos on p. 10, 33, 49, 54, 125, 136, 142, 164, 175 courtesy of Paulette Braun

Photo on p. 171 courtesy of Calida (Shutterstock)

Photo on p. 75 courtesy of James Stuart Griffith (Shutterstock)

Photo on p. 38 courtesy of Cindy Haggerty (Shutterstock)

Photo on p. 45 courtesy of HTuller (Shutterstock)

Photo on p. 146 courtesy of Dee Hunter (Shutterstock)

Photos on p. 57, 109, courtesy of Eric Isselee (accent over second 'e') (Shutterstock)

Photos on p. 95, 134, 162, courtesy of Erik Lam (Shutterstock)

Photo on p. 69 courtesy of Scott Lomenzo (Shutterstock)

Photo on p. 169 courtesy of Mike Ludkowski (Shutterstock)

Photo on p. 47 courtesy of Randy McKown (Shutterstock)

Photo on p. 197 courtesy of Steven Pepple (Shutterstock)

Photo on p. 127 courtesy of Photomediacom (Shutterstock)

Photo on p. 187 courtesy of Allyson Ricketts (Shutterstock)

Photo on p. 195 courtesy of Nicole Weiss (Shutterstock)

Photo on p. 56 courtesy of Lisa F. Young (Shutterstock)

All other photos courtesy of Isabelle Francais and TFH archives